Acknowledgements

To all my compatriots in the Family Division, I
salute you and thank you for your patience and
comradeship over the years.
To my friends and family who helped by reading
the first draft of the self help book, I thank you and
will embarrass you by naming you:
Alan, Nancy, Karen, Stan, George and Steve.
To Morgan, thank you for your help and editing
skills.
To Travis, thank you for being you.
All of you give me strength and hope.

Divorce with Dignity

CHAPTER ONE

Samantha awoke in the near dark. Or at least that would be John Steinbeck's description. Her hand reached over to Benjamin's pillow, stroking the the now cool spot his head vacated earlier. Benjamin was off to the club for his early morning workout before the beginning of the work day. She saw the empty chair on his side of the bed that last night held his workout bag with his business suit draped over the chair back. Yep, he was gone and the second alarm, the six-thirty-get-up-and-get-ready-Samantha alarm, had not yet gone off.

Samantha waited for the alarm even though she was fully conscious and ready to leave the bed. Her day did not officially start until the 6 AM alarm and Morning Edition crackled out of her clock-radio's speakers. She began her stretches as soon as her feet hit the floor. By now the exercises were part warm-up for the day, part see if she could still reach the floor in a single spine-ache-free bend. She then entered their private bathroom, the dream room she and Ben had specially

designed when their McMansion was built. The overly
large and ostentatious house was not her idea. She had
her eye on a beautiful Victorian in the village section of
town. But Ben overruled her, wanting to flex his money
for the world to see. So they found an architect and
spent months pouring over designs and plans, including
a state-of-the-art bathroom and shower, found only in the
most exclusive hotels and homes of the rich and famous.

A hot shower would get her going, ready to
take on the challenge of waking Cynthia and Edward
and begin the daily negotiations, struggles, and outright
battles that were the daily drama of getting them to
school. Getting those beloved children out of the house
was like dragging body bags through calf-deep
molasses. This was the part of the day she loathed and
would have avoided altogether if their township had no
penalties for truancy and excessive absences.

True to form, the kids groaned and pulled the
covers over their faces when Samantha nudged them
awake. Edward barely responded, the slow blinking of
his eyes and shuffling further into his warm cocoon of
bedding the only proof the he was not in some sort of
prolonged state of hibernation. Cynthia growled from her

cave, clearly agitated that her territory had been invaded. Just once Samantha wished her kids would leap out of bed, spring into their clothes, arrive at the breakfast table and have a civilized conversation with her. Just once.

Instead Samantha stood at the foot of the stairs, urging them to get ready, swearing mild (some not so mild) oaths to herself as they delayed and stalled, stalled and delayed. She couldn't come up with a sufficiently threatening threat since the "I'll tell your father" gambit always backfired. Promising the wrath of Khan if her kids didn't get downstairs at once only made them laugh since they knew Khan died in the movie and it was, well, a movie...

She made them peanut butter toast, knowing that breakfast would be eaten in the car on the way to school. She looked around the family room area, trying to spot shoes and backpacks that her kids were incapable of finding without a major scene. She looked on the refrigerator for permission slips that needed signing for that day. She made sure Edward's saxophone case was in the car so she would not get one of those annoying midday calls to bring the sax to school. She tried to remain the cool collected mother she had hoped to be - hoped to be until the first one, Cynthia, hit high school. Now it was her or them.

Her progeny finally made it downstairs, shoes on feet and backpacks on backs. Samantha handed each the lunch money they needed to add to their accounts. Unlike some other schools in the area, the kids didn't pay on a daily basis, but had a lunch slush fund that needed to be periodically revived with fresh funds. The unfortunate part of the lunch program was that she received no itemization from the school about foods eaten; she had to trust the accounting her children gave her at the end of the day.

The ride to school was always a tense one as Samantha waited for one child or the other to suddenly remember that a paper was due, homework had been assigned, or that they had to stay late for a practice or club meeting. Cynthia was of an age where she and her girlfriends liked to hang out at the local Galleria, window shopping and Starbucks loitering. Their discussions focused on the latest fashion mistake a classmate made or the latest teaching disaster.

Edward, on the other hand, did not hang around the mall after school, but was always at a band practice. If it wasn't marching band, it was concert band. If it wasn't concert band, it was jazz band. Cynthia was happy her son had an activity he enjoyed, even if it put her taxiing services on a full time basis. It also usually meant providing rides for some of Edward's band friends whose parents were at work and unable to pick up their children. She didn't mind and in fact enjoyed the kids' chatter about their day. She felt more in the loop.

And so Samantha began another day, taxiing both kids to school, an easy task now that they were both at the high school. She gave them a cheery wave with a "love you" that sometimes was returned if no one was around. She then went home to feed Scotty the terrier and Ann the Airedale before beginning her morning chores of laundry and vacuuming. With two dogs and two teenagers the carpets were always dirty. Housework - the bane of her existence. Housework was the cost of exchanging her life as an executive for a life as a homemaker.

After finishing her chores, watching Good Morning America and dressing up in preparation for going out, she heard the garage door open. "This is weird," Samantha thought as she heard Ben's familiar footsteps coming up the stairs into the house. She finished throwing on her clothes and scampered downstairs where she found him sitting in the living room. After inviting her to sit, Ben began his rehearsed speech, the one that would leave Samantha hollow and devastated.

CHAPTER TWO

Samantha awoke in the near dark. Her hand reached out across the bed and slapped the pillow where Ben's head had lain two weeks ago. She looked at the clock and realized that for once she had gotten a full night's sleep and felt somewhat refreshed from another night alone. Day 14 and Ben was still gone, moved out into a local hotel until he could find a suitable apartment.

Ben's talk reflected the shallowness of Ben-ness. Samantha was sure Ben's talk had been easier for him than he had thought. The obvious days of rehearsal had clearly paid off especially when his natural acting talents had kicked in. It's me, not you; it's a good change for both of us; yes, there's someone else; okay she's younger than you, but that's not what matters; blah, blah, blah. The kids will be okay and you're a terrific mother. I want to still be a part of their lives. We'll tell them together tonight after dinner. And so the drama that was to become her new life began for Samantha.

Samantha made a conscious effort each day to appear as normal as possible to the children. She made the same efforts to get them out of bed, fed and off to school. On weekends she would taxi them to their usual haunts, cheerfully waving them off at the mall or the movies or school functions. She concentrated on maintaining normalcy, whatever that was, for them, and not to be one of those pathetic women who curl up and hibernate in their bedrooms, neglecting children and normal obligations, requiring the care of friends or family. She would not do that to them.

Once the shock wore off, Samantha began confiding in friends. She avoided her family, a group she was sure would have voted to keep Ben in the family and kick her out if given a chance. She never felt close enough to her mother or sisters to confide in them. She *knew* they waited for every opportunity to point out her personal faults and failures. This would be great fodder for them and she saw no need to arm their arsenal.

So when her best friend Jordan invited her over for coffee after dropping off the kids, she was more than ready to unload on a sympathetic ear. Jordan and she

had been friends since college, both good looking and

flirtatious, winning the attention of more than one young

man. Both their husbands came from their college days

and they were both married within 6 months of each

other. Their children's birthdays dovetailed nicely and

the families had grown up together. They were there for

each other during all the important events: deaths of

fathers, marriages and childbirths.

Now Samantha was entering the latest phase of

so many adult lives – divorce. Jordan listened with her

usual interest as Samantha related the events of the

past two weeks. When Samantha stopped, exhausted

by the effort of revealing how horrific life had become,

Jordan stared off in the distance.

"So this is it... this is what happens after, what,

19 years of marriage? You must be devastated.." Jordan

was clearly grasping for words, stating the obvious as if

Samantha's tear strained face wasn't enough evidence.

The only thing Jordan seemed to be able to say at that

moment with complete sincerity was that she was, "so

sorry" as she poured mugs of coffee for them. pro*blem*

"Yeah, well, it's been tough. My major problem is that I want to choke the life out of him and the bitch he's with, but I don't want to be *that* woman." Samantha blew on her cup, warmed by holding the steaming mug.

Ah, "that woman," a phrase Jordan's psychological training could latch onto. "What woman do you want to be?" Jordan began employing the socratic questioning psychobabble she had mastered.

"I want...I want... I don't know, but I know I don't want to become pathetic and annoying to my friends. I don't want to hear 'poor Samantha' every time I walk into a room. I don't want people to run from me or turn away because they expect to hear me bash Ben. And I don't want people to run to me, hoping to hear me bash Ben. I want my kids to be okay, and not some pathetic children of divorce. Mostly, I don't want to talk about any of this. I don't want a shrink...no offense Jordan... I just want to be okay." Samantha took a deep breath and began sipping her coffee, hoping she didn't sound as maniacal as she felt.

"Has it occurred to you that you're going to be okay?"

Divorce with Dignity
Kathleen Berge Entenmann

"I'm not sure I deserve to be okay." The words started to get caught in Samantha's throat when the tears started. "I don't know what I did to deserve this. I feel I've let down the kids... my mother will love this... I don't know how to tell her... Everything is going to be different...I'm scared." Her thoughts and emotions tumbled out in a disorganized jumble. She noticed a drop of coffee sliding down the mug and dabbed at it with her napkin.

"Why don't you deserve to be okay?" Jordan resumed her socratic questioning, helpful in getting past the awkward emotional outburst.

"Because I failed. The most important thing I had to do was keep this family together and I failed. That makes me a failure. We don't forgive failures, Jordan."

"Of course we do. Half the judges in this county wouldn't have been elected if we didn't forgive failures. Divorcees, alcoholics, philanderers, incompetents... If the public didn't forgive these shortcomings, there would be no one on the bench."

"The public doesn't know about their shortcomings."

Divorce with Dignity
Kathleen Berge Entenmann

"Then why are you so certain they'll know about yours? And if they do, why would they care?"

"I don't know who'll know. I just believe that everyone I see will be saying behind my back 'There goes Samantha, that pathetic loser.' Worse yet, they'll be saying things about the kids, pitying them for their parents' shortcomings. You know, the sins of the parents..."

" Are not necessarily visited on the children. You're going to be okay. It's just going to take time.'

"Please don't say time heals all. Do not say time heals all. I'm not certain anything is going to make this better, even time." Samantha balled up her paper napkin into her fist.

"So you don't want to talk to a shrink and you don't want this information made public. But Samantha, you do need help. May I make a suggestion?"

"As long as it doesn't involve a shrink or talking to someone else. This is hard enough without making my life public fodder for the gossips in this town."

"Go to the bookstore. Go to the self-help section. There must be a bazillion books on getting a divorce. Find one. Buy it. Use it."

"Jordan, you know how I feel about self-help books. They're all a crock."

"I agree there are plenty of bad ones out there. Look through them and find the one that speaks to you. The right book will find you. You might not follow all the advice in it, but it's a start. And I'm not saying this because people say this, but if you need anything, just call. Not that you will. Sometimes you're so.."

"Stubborn?" Samantha offered.

"No, German. You are your heritage. You're the most German person I know, Samantha. You don't talk about your feelings, and you don't show your weaknesses. Are you the love child of Adolph and Eva?"

"Sometimes I wonder," Samantha ruefully stated, visions of her childhood dancing before her. "I wonder."

CHAPTER THREE

Samantha woke in the near dark and sighed. Another day, another bout of loneliness, despair and constipation. Since Ben's announcement, she found that no amount of fiber in combination with hot coffee would relieve the growing knot in her stomach that was part righteous indignation, part anxiety and part, well, plain old constipation. Ah, to be as regular as the laxative commercials promised.

It would have been easy to hit the laxative aisle in the drug store. Her mother was a big believer in some nightly laxatives and the occasional enema to clean out the bowels. Samantha had long ago vowed not to go that route as an adult and to replace all the processed foods her mother fed her with vegetables, fruits and whole grains. Even the occasional treat was taken in moderation. Now she found herself craving a huge hunk of rare porterhouse chased down by a six pack of Samuel Adams topped off with two containers of Chunky Monkey. Yummmm.

Divorce with Dignity
Kathleen Berge Entenmann

Since it was Saturday, Samantha awoke to an
empty house. The children were spending the weekend
at Ben's new condo, the one that convinced his lawyer
that Ben had enough disposal income to continue
making the mortgage payments on the marital house,
pay interim alimony as well as child support until a more
permanent arrangement could be reached. While
pleased with the current financial arrangement which
permitted her and the children to continue their lives with
the least disruption, Samantha knew some serious
changes were headed her way, including replacing her
affable, but somewhat clueless lawyer.

Jordan's advice about the self-help book had
gone unheeded for the past few weeks (there was
always something happening that prevented a trip to the
bookstore).
But she made up her mind that today would be the day
to hit the local bookstore and search the self-help
section for the right book. Just as soon as she
showered, ate, cleaned, fed the dogs...maybe she'd
have the energy to get her life in order.

Three hours of procrastination later, finally
showered, fed, and chores accomplished, Samantha

decided to head to the local bookstore. Even if she found all the self-help books laughably inadequate, she could still pick up a good murder mystery. Maybe she could get her undetected revenge if she read the right book.

Entering the store, she gazed at the neatly arranged rows of books and the overhead banners proclaiming the genres of the various sections. Tempted to start with unsolved murder mysteries, she persisted until she found the self-help section, conveniently located near the restrooms in case she needed to hurl after reading bad advice.

The breadth of the section was staggering - everything from curing anorexia to overcoming xenophobia filled the aisle. She was tempted to read both the anorexia as well as xenophobia books in hopes of finding people with problems bigger than hers. A little schadenfreude might feel good about now. But she persisted until she found the divorce section and pulled out a possible winner.

Divorce with Dignity. "Hmmm," Samantha mused, "an interesting concept. This could be what I need. Let's see how dorky this writer is."

The introduction to the book persuaded her that she must be in the right book.

INTRODUCTION: WHO MAY NOT BENEFIT FROM THIS BOOK

WARNING: YOU MAY BE SPENDING YOUR MONEY AND TIME ON SOMETHING FROM WHICH YOU CANNOT BENEFIT. READ THIS SECTION BEFORE PROCEEDING FURTHER!

Samantha was intrigued. "A book that warns you not to buy it. I've gotta see what's next."

Samantha read through the introductory paragraphs. The author, K. B. L., was a woman lawyer who not only practiced domestic relations law, but was going through a divorce herself. She knew the problems of divorce from both a legal and non-legal standpoint. She understood divorce from a personal and professional viewpoint. And she seemed to have a sense of humor. Good. Game on.

Divorce with Dignity
Kathleen Berge Entenmann

So what was the dignity this author was offering? A dictionary definition followed of "bearing, conduct or manner indicative of self-respect, formality or gravity." She always considered her conduct to be indicative of self-respect, but lately she felt that self-respect eroding. Could she get that back? If for no other reason could she do that for her children?

Ah, a quiz. Love quizzes. Where would the world be without quizzes? *Cosmo* couldn't function without its sex quizzes.

PLEASE ANSWER THE FOLLOWING QUESTIONS TRUTHFULLY AND TO THE BEST OF YOUR ABILITY. REMEMBER, THERE ARE NO RIGHT ANSWERS AND THIS QUIZ HAS ABSOLUTELY NO SCIENTIFIC BASIS AND VERY LITTLE MEANING.

"Okay... here goes nothing."

1. When you are eating dinner at a fine restaurant and stare at your water glass, which of the following do you see?

a. The glass is half empty.

b. The glass is half full.

c. The glass has a tiny chip in the rim and if I bring this

to the waiter's attention and complain loudly enough,

I may get a free dessert.

d. I'm too busy having a good time with my companions

to stare at the water glass.

e. The glass is always full because in really fine

restaurants the bus personnel fill the glasses

constantly.

" I like c but I guess I do have to go with e.."

2. When you are leaving a parking garage during rush

hour traffic, you always

a. Wait patiently for traffic to stop so you can pull safely

onto the street

b. Pick on the most expensive car coming down the

street and dart in front of it on the theory that the driver

won't want to wreck his or her car in a fender bender

and will therefore stop for you

c. Lay on your horn in an effort to force drivers to stop

and let you in their lane

d. Lay on the horn, give an elderly woman the finger and then just pull into traffic

e. You make it a point to never leave town during rush hour traffic

"Ben makes it a point never to leave during rush hour, but I guess that was for other reasons. I like the thinking behind b...

3. You go to the florist to order flowers for your mother for her birthday. The clerk behind the counter is on the phone with her best friend, discussing last night's episode of *Gray's Anatomy* including all the medical jargon from the show. You have to leave the shop in ten minutes in order to be on time for your lawyer. You decide to

a. Politely interrupt the clerk and ask for assistance in placing your order

b. Wait until the clerk is finished with her phone call and then tell her you really didn't mind waiting while she talked to her friend

c. Leave the store vowing never to return

d. Leave the store **loudly** vowing never to return

e. You never go to the florist to order flowers for your

mother since she is allergic to just about every kind of

vegetation on the planet which is why you grew up

never eating salads.

"What about never going to the florist because I order

everything online? Is shoving the phone down the

clerk's throat an option? Okay, d."

4. You arrive at the gym (or club for those of you who

have too much money to go to a gym) for your weekly

racquetball game with your best friend. Your best

friend arrives with cold symptoms and a low grade

fever. You decide to

a. Console your friend and decide to go to a local diner

(or the club restaurant) for a hot bowl of chicken

noodle soup

b. Tell your friend that it's okay that you not play, but

your friend has suffered a forfeit and your lifetime

record is now 157-132.

c. Insist that your friend suit up and be on the court in

ten minutes.

d. Insist that your friend suit up and be on the court in

ten minutes, **dammit**.

e. You are non-athletic and wouldn't be caught in either
gym or club.

"Option d sounds like Ben... I'm more a. I think I would
rather have the soup than play."

5. You are twenty minutes away from the arrival of your

spouse and spouse's boss whom you are entertaining

with a dinner party when you discover that your oven

is broken and the prime rib you thought was cooking

for the past two hours is stone cold. You

a. Sob hysterically for the next twenty minutes, answer

the door red-eyed and maniacal looking and tell them

you just received a phone call that your brother who

has been on safari in Kenya was reported missing and

feared trampled by a stampede of wildebeests. Under

the circumstances, you regretfully must cancel dinner.

b. Quickly call and make reservations for a fine restaurant where the bus personnel constantly fill the water glasses.

c. Tell your spouse's boss the truth, describing your past adventures with your outdated oven and have everyone laughing at this misadventure.

d. Quickly call for take out and pass the food off as your own.

e. Hate to cook, would never think of inviting your spouse's boss to your home and don't eat red meat.

"I like to think I'm c, but I'd probably try to pull off a d."

6. Your best friend whose car is in the garage for two weeks for body work following an accident has borrowed your car for the afternoon and is now calling you from the same body shop with the upsetting news that, yes indeed, there's now been an accident with your car and the mechanic's estimate is $1500 for repairs. You have a $500 deductible on your policy and your friend is broke from paying for the last accident. You

Divorce with Dignity
Kathleen Berge Entenmann

a. Scream obscenities into the phone for a solid five minutes at the top of your lungs, vowing to kill your friend.

b. Reassure your friend that shit happens, it's only a car, it's only money and you've been thinking about going green and using public transportation.

c. Immediately hang up the phone and call your lawyer.

d. Cry inconsolably for several minutes while your friend listens to your sobs in one ear and the din of machines scraping metal in the other.

e. Don't own a car an would never think of lending it to anyone if you did.

"Ben would kill me if I loaned our car and someone wrecked it. Especially if it were his brother Len. I'd probably be b, though. Thoughtful Sam."

7. Although you've made every effort to conceal your whereabouts from high school classmates, you receive an email from the chairman of your 25th reunion, informing you that the big reunion is four months from now. You

a. Graciously accept the invitation and offer to help with decorations

b. Tell this person that you never liked high school and wouldn't think of spending a minute of your time or dime of your money on attending

c. Tell this person who paraded around high school like God's gift to (name it: cheerleading, football, men, women, humanity) you really never liked him or her and wouldn't think of spending a minute of your time or dime of your money on attending

d. That while the prospect of getting together with the "old gang" is soooooo appealing, you really must beg off since you're already booked to go to the induction ceremonies for the Rock and Roll Hall of Fame since you'll be producing the show for VH1.

e. You don't own a phone and your high school never holds reunions

"Facebook is a bitch. They've already found me. I guess I'm a, even though I'd really like to tell off some of those creeps. "

Samantha looked for more questions, but instead found the following.

Now that you've completed this quiz, please total the number of a's, b's, c's. d's and e's on a piece of paper. Now fold this paper in half lengthwise and again lengthwise. Take the paper to the nearest trash receptacle and carefully and respectfully place it inside. If you have done all this in the spirit in which it was intended, you probably should continue to read this book since you re certainly not humor impaired. If you did this angrily and with malicious thoughts towards the author, please put this book down now (slowly, gently) and reach for another self-help guide on anger management. If you did all this because you believe that you were commanded to do so and had no will to disobey, please purchase this book as well as a self-help guide on becoming more assertive and taking control of your life.

"Okay, I'm somewhat amused. This isn't going to be as bad as I thought. The quiz is cute and the instructions

27

somewhat cloying, but I can read this. At least it isn't as preachy as I thought these books would be."

Seriously, now that I've had my fun, let's discuss who may not **benefit** from this book. Naturally, I would like everyone who is going through the process of divorce to read this book and take away some grain of truth or goodie that will comfort, console or assist in the process. (You've probably caught on by now that it's an unwritten law that lawyers have to write in threes).

"Amen to that. Ben can't talk in simple sentences without using a minimum of three words to state one thing."

I have constructed a list of those who probably will not benefit from this book unless they're able to change their underlying conditions. They are, and in no particular order:

- The chronically morose
- The chronically mean-spirited
- The chronically bitchy
- The chronically power hungry
- The chronically spineless

- The chronically unforgiving
- The chronically selfish.
- The chronically dependent.
- The chronically distraught.
- The chronically humor impaired.

The chronically morose. For the chronically morose, the glass is not half-empty, it's not even there or if it's there it's cracked down the middle and water is pouring all over your lap. These are individuals who no matter how good life gets will never find happiness. I think that part of this comes from an expectation of happiness that's unattainable, sort of the perfect state of happiness that exists in some theoretical and philosophical world but in real life is almost achieved through an overdose of really fine chocolate ice cream.

"Amen to chocolate, the base of the food pyramid," Samantha thought.

The chronically morose also don't believe themselves worthy of experiencing happiness. They probably entered marriage not because of some deep abiding love but with the idea that this is as good as it will get even if it's pretty crappy. The chronically morose oftentimes have a sincere sense of loyalty and duty and probably will end up marrying the person they've been dating long term for fear of breaking that person's heart at the sacrifice of personal fulfillment. The chronically morose are basically no fun and may suffer from chronic humor impairment as well as chronic spinelessness.

"Chronically morose - Ken's wife, Lenore. What an Eeyore she is. She's never happy. I don't know who settled for whom in that marriage. I always thought Ken had so much going for him and the marriage made no sense. I'll be glad not to spend holidays at her house ever again. What a blessing."

The chronically mean-spirited. Refer to the quiz. If you had the following answers, you fit this category: 2d, 3d, 4c, 4d, 6a, 6c and 7c. While some other answers may seem mean-spirited such as declaring the forfeit and announcing the lifetime record to your sickly friend in #4, this may also be done with a somewhat puckish sense of humor to alleviate the sting. Giving the finger to an old lady, however, is simply unforgivable.

What makes people mean-spirited? There are only a bizillion reasons and we all know them. It's not comforting knowing the reasons, however, when you're on the receiving end of this person's abuse. If your spouse fits this category, you may not only need this book, but some psychological and/or spiritual counseling to deal with the emotional wreckage as well as the enormous temptation to strangle the last breath from your abuser.

"Ben's Aunt Ida - how mean spirited can one person be? She never has a good thing to say about anyone, especially Ben's mother, Hilda. Never seeing her again will be a blessing."

The chronically bitchy. This person is quite a few steps below the chronically mean-spirited, but can, from time to time, exhibit those qualities as well. While this person is seldom satisfied with their lot in life, unlike the chronically morose, the bitchy do not suffer in silence.

Oh no. They make sure that every day, in every way,

their whining, sniveling and sniping infiltrate every

particle of their partner's life. Nothing is so small or

insignificant that it can pass

without comment. And even when they are trying to be

gracious and charming, they allow in just enough venom

to poison the sweetest of remarks. If you answered b or

c to question 7, you most likely fit this category. Unless

the reunion coordinator who phoned you savagely

betrayed you in high school by trying to steal your steady

while you were at home with an ACL tear in your right

knee, the outburst is uncalled for. Not that I would know

anything about that.

Hilda - there's a first class bitch. I don't think we

saw eye-to-eye about anything. She's always

complaining about my housekeeping, my cooking, my

parenting. She always makes snide comments about my

appearance, the kids' clothes, everyone's appearance.

You'd think she was part of the fashion police, parenting

police, lifestyle police. Thank God, no more dinner discussions about death, disease and taxes. Not seeing her again will be a blessing.

The chronically power hungry. This may be the only person who can effectively deal with the chronically bitchy or mean-spirited, since this person is so Machiavellian in nature that they steam roll over everyone in pursuit of their own wants. This is the person who would not be satisfied with the forfeit in racquetball, but would insist on playing the game against a sick opponent. Hey, a win is a win. Whether male or female, this person suffers from testosterone poisoning and may require hormone therapy.

"Power hungry Nick. He's the only person I know who stands up to Ida and Hilda. I'm surprised he isn't running the world by now. I can't imagine him reading and taking anyone else's advice. At least he's a good financial manager. I better snag him before Ben does."

The chronically spineless. This is the person who took my advice on grading the quiz and also needs a book on self-assertiveness training. This person has been so dominated by life that when in a bad marriage they will accept any deal, make any compromise, withstand any humiliation. They simply can't say no. If you feel yourself to be weak-willed and too easily put upon by others, if anyone has told you to grow a pair, pay special attention to Steps 6 and 7 on hiring a lawyer and counselor. You will need an excellent one of each.

"Chronically spineless - long suffering Ruth. Do this, do that, Ruth. Wouldn't say shit if she had a mouthful of it, Ruth. Thank God I'm not Ruth. But aren't we all partly Ruth? Why can't I mouth off to rude people? Thanks for the bad service - may I have more?"

The chronically unforgiving. These are the persons who refuse to get over and beyond whatever real or perceived wrong was committed against them. In a divorce proceeding, they can be discussing a proposed property settlement with their lawyer and suddenly lapse

34

into a diatribe about what a rotten person their spouse is.

Their inability to deal with necessary issues, and instead,

focus on the constant blame game poses a major

stumbling block to their attorney. Hard to get things

done if the client is mentally and emotionally

AWOL.

This person does not relent; marital misconduct

is unforgiven. Everyday social miscues such as dinner

not on time, toilet seat up, children not behaving, dog

wetting the bedroom carpet, are constant fodder for

emotional badgering and nagging. This person refuses

to live with mistakes and refuses to accept others'

repentance.

Perhaps worse than being unable to forgive

others is the inability to forgive oneself. Many who are

chronically unforgiving of others are also guilty of this.

This is a dangerous condition because in order to

effectively negotiate and treat others with dignity, you

must be able to treat yourself with dignity as well. You

can't if you can't forgive your own transgressions. Pay

special attention to Steps 1 and 2.

"Reverend Dick - the most unforgiving person I

know. His name says it all. The older kids at church call

him "Dick the Prick." He has to be a graduate of the

"We're Holier than Thou" seminary. I may have to

rethink church now. I'm sure Reverend Dick will not

have positive things to say about this divorce. Maybe

he'll even side with Ben; he does come across as a

chauvinist. He'll tell me this is my fault. It's probably my

fault. Crap."

The chronically selfish. Think of a two year old

grown to adult size with the same emotional maturity.

The entire universe revolves around this person. This

person may also suffer from the chronic bitchiness and

power hungry syndromes as well.

But the major problem with this person going

through a divorce is that their selfishness acts as a

hindrance to effective legal representation. It's also a

major stumbling block in effective negotiation, especially

when the selfishness becomes fixated on one point or proposal creating a stalemate.

Another major stumbling block to this person's personal growth is a lack of generosity of spirit. This lack manifests itself in a failure to be able to wish the other spouse good things in life. This lack of nobility of spirit and character can result in a life filled with bitterness.

The chronically dependent. A good friend of mine from lifetime ago had a mother who fit this category. This woman was incapable of doing anything for herself. She refused to drive thereby making any licensed adult her chauffeur. She refused to stay in her house alone when her husband went on business trips. She refused to attempt even the most minor repairs such as changing a light bulb or plunging a toilet. Her favorite thing to make for dinner was reservations.

Adding to her debilitating dependency was her hypochondriasis. Those who were responsible for driving her about soon learned where her doctors were located as this was a frequent trip. Throughout this insanity her husband would either battle with her or ignore her, but fortunately never divorced her. Had it come to that she would have become the mother of all basket cases.

All of us are dependent on others to some extent or another. In a marriage, seldom re both people so self-sufficient that the other's absence would go unnoticed. Husbands and wives both tend to become dysfunctional in their ability to handle the most routine of household tasks when the other is absent. But the chronically dependent becomes hopelessly dysfunctional when faced with the permanent dissolution of the marriage.

"Selfish and dependent? Sounds like little sister Frances. I wonder if she's learned to change a light bulb or deal with mice and ants. I've never met someone so self-centered that she thought nothing of ordering others around to fetch her tissues when she sneezed and

Oreos when she craved them. I don't miss being around that. The wonder is that she ever got married."

The chronically distraught. Not a day goes by without the chronically distraught individual emoting over the lost marriage. This can be for public display, especially if their personality contains a hint of chronically bitchy. It can also be internalized as in the case of the chronically spineless. As with other major personality disorders (which have been grossly generalized and simplified above) the chronically distraught are again a hindrance to their own recovery and the ability of their attorney to represent them effectively.

Chronically distraught - our neighbor Nell. I've never seen the proverbial chicken without its head, but that's Nell. She's a trauma waiting to happen. She's a drama in need of a stage.

The chronically humor impaired. Those who have not chuckled, laughed or even smirked at this book so far, suffer from this condition. Read no further because it doesn't get much better. It's all pretty much on this level.

"Humor impaired - Ben? No, not Ben. At least he makes me laugh. Made me laugh. Made me cry..."

Samantha ended her inventory of family, friends and acquaintances, categorizing them according to their personality traits. She found herself in part in every category, but not to the chronic extent.

In all seriousness, although I have grossly oversimplified and generalized the major personality disorder who may not benefit from reading this book, I trust that each of you has seen a glimpse (come on, be honest) of yourself in these descriptions. If you haven't seen yourself, perhaps the image of your spouse has come leaping off the page and you've recognized a key problem that aided in the destruction of your marriage. Read on and learn how you can deal more effectively with your estranged spouse and with the world in general by maintaining your dignity. On the other hand, if you don't mind being the butt of every office joke, playing the part of the shrew or insanely jealous and offended

spouse, good luck, God bless, and I hope you already

paid for this copy.

"What the hell. Where's the cashier. Let me get

this and get the new life started."

Chapter Four

Samantha awoke in the near dark, panicked that she may have forgotten to set her clocks back an hour. She turned on the radio and listening for a local newscast and the time. 6:45 - plenty of time to get ready for Sunday school and church. Oddly refreshed after a day of self revelation inspired by her new book, she felt ready to move onward with life.

Since the kids were still with Ben, she was alone in the house. She was only responsible for herself today; no tussles over getting irritable children ready for Sunday school and church. Just Samantha. It felt strangely liberating. Time to read all the newspaper sections, do the crossword puzzles, both Chicago and NY Times. Time to fill until the kids came back from Ben's. Time alone.

After her morning stretches which now included some ab crunches and upper arm work, Samantha showered and dressed. Without the kids at home, she decided to go out for a bagel and schmear instead of making her Sunday morning pancakes and eggs. Going to a Presbyterian church always seems more palatable when combined with a stop at a Jewish deli. Maybe some lox today.

Sunday school was the usual lecture by one of the adult wannabe ministers. Samantha wondered why these men didn't just forego their careers and enter seminary since they enjoyed flaunting their Bible knowledge in front of devout but less informed peers. The opening and closing prayers to these sessions seemed to go on forever, the teacher seeming to want to monopolize God's attention and divert it from the Lutherans or Methodists down the street. When these people were given a part in the worship service they morphed into ministers, shedding their laic identities to become another Billy Graham.

Although she and Ben had been separated for several weeks now, no one seemed to know that fact. Or maybe, no one wanted to speak with Samantha about that fact. She received the polite hellos with no inquiries as to the whereabouts of her children or Ben. She didn't expect any questions about Ben's non-appearance since he had become more of a

Presbyterian CEO: Christmas - Easter Only. The

children's attendance was reasonably regular although

of late she avoided the inevitable morning hassles with

them by going alone.

Before church Reverend Dick made it a point to

walk through the congregation, glad handing some,

joking with others, making his presence known.

Samantha always dreaded these visits, sensing the

forced sincerity on the minister's part as he greeted each

member he saw, clearly unwilling to engage in more than

a cursory hello. While she would have welcomed some

sincere interaction with her pastor, she dreaded the

questions and what she felt were accusations sure to

come from this man. His sermons clarified that he felt

homosexuality to be an abomination and abortion

blasphemy. With two children whose sexual identities

were not yet completely formed, she cringed at the

judgmental nature of it all. She cringed wondering what

Reverend Dick would make of her situation and her

family values.

This morning's sermon focused yet again on

how America was going to hell in an hand basket, the

nickname Samantha gave to the current series of diatribes on the moral decay in America. "Abortions are on the rise. This is a blasphemy against God." "News flash, pal.. abstinence isn't working and no one wants to teach birth control and lose federal funding. That kind of leaves abortion as the last alternative for pregnant teenagers who do not want babies." Samantha listened once again to the same old message, arguing against Reverend Dick in her mental debate.

At last the sermon was over, the final hymn sung (cut down to two verses, the usual when Reverend Dick went overtime) and Samantha's self imposed obligation to God was completed for another Sunday. "What do I take from this experience?" Samantha pondered. "I don't care for the minister, he apparently doesn't care for me, and everything he says makes my blood boil. WHY am I here?"

As Samantha approached the exit, she thought she had the perfect exit strategy to avoid personal exposure to Reverend Rick. "If I can just sidle past this woman who's telling him how enthralled she is with his message, I can get out of here without speaking to the man." That thought evaporated when the long arm of

Reverend Rick reached out and grasped Samantha's arm. Caught. Trapped.

"Samantha, how good to see you. Where are young Edward and Cynthia?" Reverend Rick had her in his grip, shaking her free hand with pastoral fervor.

"They're with Ben right now." Samantha hoped her reply would ward off further questioning.

"And where is Ben? I heard some talk that the two of you were separated." Reverend Dick moved in for the kill, his grip on her arm tightening.

"You heard right. We're apart." Samantha put her hand over Reverend Dick's, hoping he would release his hold on her.

"Reconciling, I hope." The pressure tightened.

"I'm not sure..." What Samantha wanted to say was "don't hold your breath" but that sounded a little too flippant a response for even a nosey minister.

"Well, you're in my prayers. If you want, I'd be happy to do some couples counseling for you two." Samantha turned her head so her eye roll went unseen when the offer was made. "Sure you want us for counseling... and what is the hourly rate?" Samantha

thought.

"Thank you for the offer, Reverend. I'm not

certain that we're good candidates." Samantha's reply

was made courteously, not voicing her brain's sarcasm.

"Well, when I saw Ben downtown this week, he

told me about the separation and how he wanted his

family back together."

Samantha tried hard not to explode. "He did, did

he? Well did he mention that he's been having an affair

with one of the young associates at his office? Did he?

Do you expect me to reconcile with that?"

"Now, now, Samantha. There are always two

sides to the story..." Reverend Rick continued with some

patronizing b.s. about how she may share in some of the

blame for the dissolution of the marriage. Samantha

knew if she listened closely she'd go postal on this man.

"So don't you agree that you owe it to the children to

reconcile with Ben?"

Ah, the guilt card. If Samantha remained firm in

proceeding with the divorce Ben filed, was she short

changing her children? Worse, was she short changing

herself?

Divorce with Dignity
Kathleen Berge Entenmann

Samantha mumbled a goodbye,removed her arm from Reverend Dick's hold and headed to her car. Never had she left church in as bad a state as today. All the guilt she was trying to rid herself of rose to the surface. Reverend Dick did one heck of a head number on her. She needed to clear her thoughts and absolve herself of further guilt.

When she got home Samantha quickly changed clothes, leashed the dogs and went outdoors for a long walk. The property abutted a nice woodland area, complete with a marked trail and stream. As soon as she was safely out of view from the neighbors, she let Scott and Ann off their leashes to run and chase small critters. She lazily tagged after them, occasionally calling them to return to her. Always shocked when the dogs actually listened to her, she lavishly rewarded them, emptying her dog treat filled pockets.

After an hour of aimless wandering, Samantha called the dogs one last time, clipped on their leashes and headed home. The cool air helped clear her head, but her heart felt the crushing weight of the shame, guilt and self pity she felt about the separation and pending divorce. She needed some guidance; maybe the book could help.

Samantha opened the refrigerator and removed the Frog's Leap chardonnay she enjoyed on the weekends. After uncorking the bottle, laughing at the "ribbitt" on the label, she poured a glass and settled in her favorite chair in the living room.

STEP ONE - FORGIVE YOURSELF

To forgive is to set a prisoner free and discover that the prisoner was

you."

Lewis B. Smedes

Let's start off with the hardest lesson of all and maybe the rest will be a breeze; forgive yourself. Take a deep cleansing breath and say out loud "I forgive myself." Do it again, this time with meaning. Come on, one more time. Feel forgiven?"

Samantha closed her eyes, stood in a relaxed yoga pose and breathed. "I forgive myself," she chanted as though it were her personal mantra. "I forgive myself....I forgive myself." Nope. Nothing changed. Did this jackass writer think it would be that easy?

This probably didn't work because one of the most difficult life tasks is learning forgiveness. It's tough enough to forgive the other guy, turn the other cheek, be the bigger person, but forgiving oneself can be Herculean. But difficult as this may be, one cannot achieve the sense of dignity we are striving for without first forgiving ourselves our own transgressions as we forgive those who transgress against us. Hence, this book is not for the chronically unforgiving, especially those who cannot forgive themselves.

Let me make myself absolutely clear on one point in this self-forgiveness step. I am not talking about absolving oneself of responsibility or ducking from the consequences of one's behavior. What I am talking about is straightforward acknowledgement of any wrongdoing, facing the fact that maybe, just maybe, we are guilty of wrongdoing, and learning to live with the consequences of our wrongdoing. If we are to have self-respect and dignity, we cannot run from the problems we create for ourselves and others. To do so is to display a breathtaking lack of integrity to others. However, if we are to function in our private and social lives, we cannot constantly engage in self-flagellation over what we have done wrong. To do so severely limits our ability to move on in life and function as we must for the sake of our families, our friends, our colleagues and ourselves.

Samantha felt better with each word. At first she thought this was going to be trite bullshit. Now she felt that some truth, however insignificant, was starting to be revealed. She knew her self-pity which was rising to the level of self-flagellation was not serving her best interests. Apparently at least one other person out there knew this too.

The first step in forgiving oneself is to remember that as powerful as you think you are, and you may be pretty powerful, you are incapable of controlling everyone and everything around you. This is one reason why the chronically power hungry will never benefit from this book and achieve dignity during divorce; they truly believe they have that power. Trust me - no one does. CEO's of major corporations, partners in large law firms, heads of state, even surgeons: no one is that powerful. So why do you think you are?

Time for another quick quiz:

1. Do you believe that if you left your teenage children alone for an entire day that they would starve to death?

2. Do you believe that it is possible for you to work full time, come home, clean house and cook dinner, and still have energy to play with your children and help them with their homework and personal chores before bedtime?

3. Do you believe that after your divorce your spouse will become a social recluse and that you are the only person capable of bringing joy into that person's life.

4. Do you believe that if you left on vacation today, with no prior notice, that the office would crumble and the business fail?

"What's with the quizzes? Is this writer a frustrated teacher? Got the point - no one will starve, I'm not Supermom, Ben's social life is much fuller than mine, and any business could survive without me."

If you answered yes to all of the above, welcome to my delusion. I am certain that life for everyone I know and have contact with would cease to continue without my presence. But I know from experience that teenagers are resourceful; they can order pizza and heat up leftovers. Unless you are on drugs, no one can work a full day, come home and do housework, and still have energy for children. Ex-spouses develop lives without you, sometimes ones more rewarding than the one you two shared. And unless you are a sole practitioner or business owner, life in the office rebounds without you. You are **not** the center of the universe and without you, while life for others may not be the same, it will be

survivable.

It's just more fun to think that it can't.

"Me? Am I the center of the universe? Is that my problem?" Samantha put the book down and considered her role in the lives of her family - her entire extended family. As middle child, she was the peacemaker between Frances, the older and Georgia, the younger. No family gathering took place unless she was the one to call everyone and mediate any disputes.

And the kids? She permitted them to use her as their backup so that forgotten books, instruments and homework could be delivered to school in time for class. She kept track of everyone's appointments, from medical to social, and made sure no one missed an engagement of any kind.

And Ben - Ben who had long had his own life, free of responsibilities for the kids. She enabled Ben to maintain his lifestyle. Already in the weeks since their separation, he asked her on a few occasions to step in and have the kids stay with her when some other commitment interfered with his custody. Of course he assumed she had nothing better to do; the kids were always her first priority.

"So screw you, Reverend Dick. Ben may feel guilty about leaving his family, but he certainly is not letting that slow down his social life." Samantha voiced aloud the resentment she harbored since church that morning. It started to feel better.

The only people who truly cannot survive without your constant love and support are your children and you. *YOU!* Every other adult out there has to be able to make it on their own. And one day, that will include your children as well. It's a scary thought, but one day your children will be leaving the nest and you will be alone.

"My head knows this. My heart refuses to accept that Edward and Cynthia will no longer need me. I wonder if dorms have rooms for moms."

Children are oftentimes the main stumbling block in obtaining self forgiveness because as parents we believe that everything we do will ultimately affect our children and that unless we pursue some fictionalized ideal of the perfect family, our children will grow up more dysfunctional than we are. We have come to believe that our children will carry emotional scars for life. We have come to believe that these scars are all our fault because we were breaking up the unified family. We have come to believe that this is a knockout punch our children can't survive. As result, we feel enormous guilt.

It helps if you realized from the time your children were born that there was nothing you could do in this lifetime them from emotional harm. You're not at the playground, in the locker room, or sitting in the cafeteria where snottiness and bullying are life events. It is also helpful to realize that no matter what you say or do your children will grow up blaming you for all the pain and inadequacies in their lives. I can't tell you how many times I've listened to adult children complain about the treatment they received at the hands of their parents. I'm not talking about legitimate abuse issues where a child was routinely physically and emotionally

beaten, or issues of neglect by self-indulgent parents.

I'm talking about adult children who felt their parents

were overly critical, overly demanding and insufficiently

affectionate. These are children who were raised very

similarly to you and me and whose parents wanted

nothing more than the best for their child and wanted

their child to achieve his or her full potential.

Now as adults, these children insist that

everything that is going wrong in their lives dates back to

the manner in which they were raised. In fact they were

raised by people who never intended harm, but did

everything they though was correct and reasonable in

raising their children.

"Sounds like Frances and Georgia, always

bitching about Mom or Dad. If it wasn't my fault, it was

our parents."

Just keep in mind that no matter how perfect you

are, no matter how good a parent you strive to be, your

children will ultimately blame you for their lot in life. If you hadn't divorced, the blame would result from some

other supposed deficiency; you were overly critical,

overly demanding and insufficiently affectionate. Don't

blame yourself for their unhappiness; you are not

perfect. You do the best you can and move on in life.

They will have to do the same.

None of this is meant to demean or belittle the

statistics that children of divorce do suffer some serious

side effects. Adult children of divorce have difficulty

entering into relationships with others, suffering from

lack of trust. Young children suffer the effects of not

seeing Mom or Dad daily and being shuttled between

two houses. But again, consider your adult friends as

well as any other children you my know. You can see

some serious emotional and mental problems in those

who came from intact families as well as those who

suffered a family breakdown. Children of divorce have

not cornered the market on emotional fallout.

Divorce with Dignity
Kathleen Berge Entenmann

"So true," Samantha thought as she thought about all her friends, especially women she knew in college. Most of them were damaged goods, happy to be away from home, trying to make a go of a relationship. Many of them found the right man or woman. Many didn't. "I thought I was set. I guess not."

Samantha read on, sipping her wine and nodding her head when the writer suggested that kids enjoy it when adults admit their imperfections. "That's Cynthia and Edward.. always ready to show me what a goof I am. They love telling me 'I told you so.' They're worse than parents at times. I keep telling myself I'm doing a good job. I keep telling myself, but I wish I knew for sure."

Samantha read on, absorbing the advice, grinning at some of the humor. Then she turned the page and read the following:

For men only: I really wasn't kidding earlier when I stated that no matter how powerful you are, you do not control your wife's happiness. it's comforting to realize that you are not totally responsible for others' happiness, even though your entire life other around you drove you to one goal: be a responsible provider for yourself and family. If you are the one who is moving for the divorce, on top of that enormous burden of responsibility, you now carry the guilt of being the cause of someone else's unhappiness. Don't act out of that guilt. More than once I've a seen a guilt ridden husband bind himself to an agreement he found impossible to fulfill. Do what is reasonable and necessary, even somewhat generous. But don't go to the extreme of cutting yourself off from even the most modest of pleasures in order to assuage your guilty conscience.

Case in point: A husband I began to represent long after his divorce and agreement were final wanted to modify his agreement that provided support for his family in the amount of 50% of his gross (**not net**) income. At first he was willing to limit his lifestyle to a studio apartment, and forego the simple pleasures of life such as an occasional movie, new clothing or a meal other than twenty-five cent boxes of macaroni and cheese. He lived life on the financial edge and nearly

committed suicide, despairing over his failed health, his

failed marriage, and what had become a failed attempt

to adequately provide for his children. Most of this was

brought on by the fact that he acted out of guilt in

entering into a bad marriage settlement agreement,

poorly drafted, with, let's say, inadequate legal advice.

Were it not for the fact that his former wife was

not only totally unsympathetic, but also totally

unappreciative of his efforts to support his family, he

would have continued to willingly abide the terms of this

one-sided agreement. Now he wanted the courts to

rewrite the support terms since the agreement was

incapable of performance unless one vows to live the life

of a secluded monk or hermit, coming out of hiding to

work a 12 hour day and then receding back into his cell.

Be honorable, be somewhat generous, but do not

engage in self-flagellation throughout this proceeding

because everyone, yourself included, perceives you to be

a bad guy. Forgive yourself and work on reaching an amicable resolution so that you and your wife can survive this divorce. Bankrupting yourself will only lead to anger and further pain down the road. Cutting yourself off from your children because an angry wife has convinced you that they would be better off without you and you feel too much guilt to fight will not serve anyone's interests either. forgive yourself and act in accordance with what is right, not what will assuage your guilty conscience.

Even if you are not the moving party in this divorce, if you are not the one who wants the family to break apart, you still experience feelings of guilt mixed in with the frustration and anger of having your life ripped apart. Forgive yourself for whatever sins you think you've committed by either driving your wife away or by failing to recognize the problems before it was too late. Act responsibly towards her and your children in reaching an amicable settlement that both of you will be able to live with.

"Forgive himself? I hope he chokes on his guilt, *if* he even feels guilty. I'd better get him into a courtroom fast - strike while the guilt is hot."

For women only: Let's face it, when it comes to family and marriage, we think we're the only ones who can keep the family together and bear the brunt of all the work, both physical and emotional. We have this inbred burden to be the creator, the comforter and the peacemaker for everyone, including our spouses. When they hurt, we hurt. And so we try to mend and heal and comfort. Oftentimes we come up short of our goal of solving the problems that plague our families and loved ones.

When we are the cause of the hurt, we feel a tremendous loss of self esteem that comes from being this almighty problem solver. We fall into cycle of self-recrimination and depression from not only being unable to solve the problems of someone in pain but also from having inflicted that pain. This burden is overwhelming at times and leads us straight into the path of the oncoming trainload of bad decisions that we think help others at the cost of our own emotional well-being.

The great liability that comes with being the creative force in a relationship, the nurturer and peacemaker, is that you don't want to inflict pain on others. This instinctive protection of others holds back many women with children from going through with a divorce, even when abuse is involved. How many of us know women who stay in abusive relationships, or even obtain protection from abuse orders and then allow their husbands to return home? After watching this pattern for years, I've concluded, after debriefing clients who have engaged in this self-destructive behavior, that they cannot stand to inflict pain on others, even when the object of that pain is their abuser. Hence, women obtain protection from abuse orders and then let the creeps back into the home because ***they*** don't want to cause

someone else pain. As long as we're needed, we put up

with all kinds of stuff. We're nuts, plain and simply.

"Feeling a bit nuts myself. This is true, so true."

Case in point. I know of a young woman whom

fortunately I don't represent, otherwise I would have her

committed for mental incompetence. Why? She and

her boyfriend began seeing an attorney a few years back

for criminal representation for various petty offenses such

as drunk and disorderly or malicious mischief, the sort of

charges one inevitably faces when your life's ambition is

drinking all day in the neighborhood bar.

Early on it was apparent that she was the victim

of some abuse; the occasional black eye or severely

bruised arm were dead giveaways. She would deny that

anything was happening and that what was happening

was not the boyfriend's fault.

Pretty soon the cuts and bruises became more

severe and she began obtaining emergency protection

from abuse (PFA) orders. The first time she got one, she actually showed up for the final hearing and obtained an order excluding the boyfriend from the apartment for two months. Of course, true love triumphed over common sense and she let him back in. Within weeks he once again beat her up, she pursued a PFA, he convinced her of his undying love, she let him back in. And so on - one vicious circle of hurt.

Too ashamed to let her attorney know what was happening, she handled the PFA actions on her own, filing and dismissing, filing and dismissing, filing and dismissing. And then one day (who doesn't see this coming) the boyfriend really beat the crap out of her. Hospitalization was required. I thought a frontal lobotomy might be appropriate to erase any notions she might have of reconciling with this monster. Happy to say, this time she stuck to her guns, obtained a PFA and pressed criminal charges.

Divorce with Dignity
Kathleen Berge Entenmann

I wondered why she felt compelled to always take him back, exposing herself to increasing levels of violence. The closest answer I arrived at was that she felt sorry for him and thought she could reform his alcoholism. She needed to nurture this jerk, even though he could only repay her with violence. She received something from this relationship that she couldn't find elsewhere in her sorry existence: a feeling of superiority and the knowledge that she was desperately needed, even if only as a punching bag.

"God. If Ben ever laid a finger on me, he'd be missing that finger - and other body parts as well. Thank God I never lived this hell."

You have to let go of the notion that you can cure all the world's ills including those inflicted upon or even caused by your children and/or spouse. You have to remind yourself that this same need to be the creator, nurturer and peacemaker for the rest of humanity is also the need that prevents you from creating, nurturing and making peace with yourself.

We find it difficult to forgive outsiders from
disrupting our homes, inflicting pain and creating havoc.
Therefore, it is so much more difficult to forgive
ourselves when we are in the role of destroyer and
disrupter since we are the creators and nurturers. In
order to survive this process and retain our self-respect,
we have to seriously rethink our roles in the family
relationship in order to get on with our life and recovery.
This can only be accomplished by genuinely forgiving
ourselves for breaching our role as wife and mother.

"I wasn't the one who destroyed this family. I'm
now going to be the ex-wife. And
it's Ben's fault."

Samantha turned to the last page. "Oh, good.
Tasks. I feel tasked enough already."

Tasks for Step One

1. Take inventory of your role in your marriage, listing
   those things you did that benefitted you and your
   spouse and those things your did that were destructive
   to the relationship. Be honest with yourself.

2. Now congratulate yourself for all the good things you accomplished. If you were honest, you will find that in many ways you were a good spouse, regardless of anything negative your spouse is saying about you now.

3. Take the list of the destructive things and one by one forgive yourself for each act. Don't destroy the list, however. You may want to refer to this in the future when you're considering remarriage.

Samantha found one of Ben's old legal pads and began to write.

Good

1. Helped Ben through law school.
2. Helped Ben's career – good lawyer's wife.
3. Raised the kids.
4. Kept in shape.
5. Kept the house
6. Put up with Ben's family and entertained them for holidays, birthdays.

7. Made sure kids had good relationship with Ben's family.

8. Gave up my career for family

As ridiculous as it felt, Samantha gave herself a pat on the back and a verbal "atta girl" for all her accomplishments. She was especially proud of her role as a full time homemaker and the way she had raised her kids. She had done well.

Destructive

1. Drove Ben nuts with spending.

2. Complained about his work hours

3. Complained about his family, especially his mother

4. Nagged him about his appearance

5. Coddled the kids too much?

6. Gave up my career for family

7.

8.

Samantha read through this list, and as ridiculous as it sounded, forgave herself out loud for each and every item. She noticed that "gave up career for family" made both lists. Why?

Chapter Five

Samantha awoke in the near dark. The clock radio began blaring the 6:00 hour of *Morning Edition*. She half-heartedly listened to the latest news of the middle East and the midwest. NPR was not inspiring her to get out of bed and *carpe diem*. I'd rather *carpe carp* - seize the carp and go fishing. But another school day beckoned her to begin the Samantha routine of getting reluctant children out of bed, out of house, out of car, and into high school.

Over the past several weeks since the separation Samantha honed the school routine until she no longer felt the overwhelming need to strangle one child or the other. Both Edward and Cynthia also felt a responsibility to cooperate with their mother who was going through a weird and stressful time. They appreciated the fact that they saw their workaholic father more now when they were apart than when he resided in the same house with them. Samantha never put up roadblocks to prevent Ben from being with his kids. And while Ben didn't give up his blackberry during his time with the kids, he was at least physically present and more engaged than in the past.

Samantha was still having problems dealing with Ben. Her problems stemmed not from an overbearing Ben; he became more compliant than he had been during the marriage. The problem was her own stubborn refusal to forgive and forget.

Samantha decided to dedicate today to reading Divorce with Dignity, hoping that she would gain an epiphany to help her get over the continuing ache. She poured a mug of fresh brewed coffee, retrieved the book and sat down in the living room, intent on concentrating on a new step.

STEP TWO: FORGIVE THE OTHER GUY

How can you display self respect when you continue to exact

revenge?

Living well is the best revenge. *Spanish proverb.* I love this proverb. Once you have committed this to your mind and heart you can forgive others and move on with your own life. You can have your Karma cake and eat it too. You can express forgiveness of others and exact

revenge from them as well. WOW!

Let's face it, even the most benign among us, the

most religious, the most pious still have an incredibly

difficult time with forgiveness. Sure, we're all taught to

do this by our parents, our religions, our communities.

And it's the one thing we're almost always incapable of

doing. If forgiving ourselves is the hardest task we face,

forgiving others ranks as number two and often closes in

on and surpasses number one as the most difficult.

How wonderful, then, to know that by

transforming your life into one in which you are living

well, that you will also have forgiven the other spouse

and exacted the best revenge. By forgiving the other

spouse, you move out of that spiteful and hateful mind

set that's incredibly unattractive to those around you.

You can then enter into a more serene state of being that

your friends, family, colleagues and potential suitors can

admire. You stop being the jealous and angry ex-spouse

whom no one wants to deal with. You become the
sadder but wiser divorcee who doesn't start every
conversation with graphic images of eviscerating your
spouse. You are thought of as courageous, sage,
empowered and just plain **nice** which is so much better
than being thought of as sniveling, dense, weak and just
plain **difficult**.

For the short run, the unforgiving, vengeful
spouse gets great play in society. In fact, your family and
friends often will encourage you to play the part because
they get the vicarious thrill of watching a real life soap
opera. You will be encouraged to "get every dime," "not
pay a penny," "destroy him," "destroy her," "make his/
her life a living hell." In the meantime, by following this
advice, you've made your life a living hell. What's the
point?

The bottom line is that as long as you're playing
out the role of the wronged spouse and plotting various
methods of revenge, you are delaying the process of

getting on with your life. Here's a suggestion to move

you along if you are still in the initial stages of shock

from this divorce: have a major gripe party with close

friends. If you received a Dear John/Jane letter as part

of the breakup, post it for others to read. This may take

some personal encouragement to get over any personal

embarrassment. Leave a pad for others to write their

snappy comebacks to your spouse. Once you've had

your cathartic exercise, take any written outpourings and

follow the directions for disposition of the quiz in the

introduction: fold and throw away in the trash. You don't

want this evidence discovered by your spouse's attorney

or a district attorney if realistic physical threats were

made.

By no means conduct this exercise via the

internet on any social network such as facebook or in a

personal blog. Judges love to read vitriolic bloggings

while judging whether or not you should have custody of

your children. Cyberbullying and threats are taken

seriously by the authorities. You don't need this kind of legal grief.

It becomes easier to forgive if you remember a few truths about any relationship. First, it's helpful to remember that you chose to marry this person in the first place. This decision was presumably a rational and sober one. Unless you were drugged or fraudulently conned into this marriage, in which you have grounds for an annulment, you wanted this partner. For life. Until death do we part. You must have had a reason.

Try and find that reason. Once you clearly remember why you married, you can concentrate on your spouse's finer qualities. Maybe you always appreciated how industrious your spouse was; you just didn't realize that this would turn into a workaholic lifestyle. Perhaps you appreciated how charming and sexy your spouse was; you didn't realize this meant philandering. Whatever the reason for the attraction, try and keep these good qualities in mind. Remembering these qualities helps when you begin the process of forgiving your spouse for their marital sins which have led to your divorce. It's far easier to forgive someone whom we can look upon without total disdain than someone we envision as Lucifer.

Caveat: Forgiveness does **not** necessarily entail **forgetting.** Focusing on your spouse's good qualities does **not** mean putting totally out of mind the bad. Some lessons should be engraved on our gray matter for life. Just because you're willing to move past the emotional, mental or even physical pain of a relationship does not mean that you forget how you got to the place you are today. Forgetting is a sure ticket to repeating the same mistakes again. I can't tell you how many times I've seen people commit the same mistakes over again. And I have to emphasize that the divorce rate goes up the more often you're married. ***Break the cycle!***

Remember what went wrong and try not to repeat the same mistake. Take a long honest look at how you chose your first mate and determine what went wrong in the selection process. Maybe you were too young and thought beauty was everything and now realize that a few more brain cells might not have hurt your spouse. Maybe you wanted someone just like Dad and found out why Mom has never been truly happy in her marriage because you're dealing with the same sort of control freak. Whatever the problem, try to make an assessment before you find yourself saying "I do" to spouse number two. Although remarriage may be the furthest thing from your mind at the moment, statistics show that the majority of divorced persons will make that trip again. Just make sure the next trip doesn't end up in a courtroom somewhere.

Second, when I wrote in Step One that you are not all powerful, the same truth applies to your spouse. Your spouse is **not** all powerful. There is no way you have lost all control over your own life unless you have been lobotomized or locked away in a tower. There may indeed be power imbalances between you and your

spouse, and there may be certain aspects of the marriage

where you lost or abdicated control to the other.

Chances are, though, that for every concession you

made, concessions were made to you. You may not have

chosen the vacation spot every year, but chances are that

if you didn't like it, you made your lack of enthusiasm

known. Not wanting to make the same mistake twice,

your spouse may have relinquished the vacation decision

to you. We exercise control in myriad ways, from

passive/aggressive to just plain aggressive.

I realize that this is not a popular notion in this

day and age of everyone being a victim. Yes, we're all

victims in some way or other, and some of us will never

overcome our victimization. Mine is being born to big

boned people who have the DNA for fat genes in their

personal chemistry. The American diet industry has

lined its pockets with the money of desperate dieters

trying to overcome genetic destiny. But victim of genetic

fat predisposition or not, your destiny is still yours to control.

Your desire to be a happy and fulfilled person can only be realized by you and not through the actions of others. Certainly others can either enhance that goal or become impediments. But in the end, if inner peace, happiness and personal fulfillment are what you seek, you'll get there despite the objections or roadblocks from others.

It's entirely natural to feel as though you can't overcome or maneuver past these roadblocks, but it's imperative to get back into control. As discussed above, have your cathartic experience and let out the venom. Once you've gone through this exercise, don't repeat it. Start by making a conscious effort not to cave into the inner voice of temptation or the cajoling of others to speak ill of the departed spouse. Employ the basic lesson taught by every elementary or Sunday school teacher; if you can't say something nice, don't say anything at all.

Divorce with Dignity
Kathleen Berge Entenmann

Believe me, this is extremely difficult advice to follow during times of enormous stress, especially when you wish with every fiber of your physical and psychic being that you could emotionally, mentally and sometimes physically rip the other spouse to shreds and send tiny fragments of their mental and corporeal being floating into the cosmos. If this becomes an overwhelming compulsion, use every creative power at your command to mentally and non-verbally destroy this person. Once you've exorcised the demons seeking revenge, obtain the ultimate in revenge: **Forgive the lowlife!**

Why forgive? By not forgiving the lowlife, you will encounter tremendous difficulties in achieving an intimate and sustaining relationship with another partner. More than one client has remarked to me that during and after divorce, they were having difficulty dating. Why? Trust was difficult to develop with someone new because they were still so wounded and hurt from the first marriage. One client actually experienced a rude awakening when a rather long term relationship fell apart because his girlfriend was so put off by the venomous feelings he had for his ex-wife. You do not make yourself lovable to a new potential mate or companion by showing how psychotic you become if the relationship falls apart.

As with everything that's difficult to accomplish in life, once the task of forgiving your spouse has been undertaken and successfully completed, you will be a better person. Honest, your mother, father, teacher, preacher didn't lie about this. You find strength you never knew you had, be it strength of character or the strength to physically restrain yourself from punching out someone else's lights. You enter into a state of grace by realizing that you have resisted temptations that seemed overwhelming. You battled your personal demons and won. Your soul is better for the experience.

***The ultimate step in forgiveness: Make
friends with your ex-spouse.***

Now that you're done laughing at this suggestion, let's
talk seriously. You've mentally and perhaps verbally
emasculated your ex-husband. You've mentally and
perhaps verbally abused your
ex-wife. You've said nasty things and in some moments
of insanity, committed them to writing. I have no
illusions that just by writing this book I've prevented any
of this from happening. I just hope that whatever has
happened hasn't been taken to the extremes where
criminal proceedings are initiated.

Why be friends? Isn't that the worst breakup
line in the book? "I don't love you, but can't we still be
friends?" People retch when they hear that in movies or
in real life. The line is generally met with universal
rejection and the snappy comeback "when hell freezes
over" or some such vituperative comment.

Divorce with Dignity
Kathleen Berge Entenmann

Being friends doesn't mean that the two of you meet once a week for coffee or lunch and share your life experiences, but in some cases, it might. It doesn't mean that every time you have a crisis you turn to each other, but in some cases it might. It might mean something as simple as wishing each other well, even though your ex-spouse has caused enormous hurt.

Friends respect and care for each other. Friends do not engage in conduct that is destructive or vindictive. Friends support each other. Friends wish each other well.

Now is the time to go back to that storeroom of memories and find the reasons why you cared for this person in the first place. List all the positive attributes that attracted you. Remember these.

Doing this will help you bury the anger and frustration that will hinder you from getting o with your life. Doing this will display your character that is worthy of respect from other. Doing this will display your self-respect.

Remember the Spanish proverb, "Living well is the best revenge." Living without taking revenge, wallowing in hurt and spewing it back is also living well. And that's the best revenge.

Tasks for Step Two

1. Make a list of all the reasons and qualities that attracted you to your spouse prior to marriage. Evaluate your spouse currently to see if any of these reasons or qualities still exist.

2. Practice a civil conversation to have with your spouse in the event that the two of you still see each either, either through social, business or family connections. Even if the conversation consists simply of "Hi, how are you?", practice saying it without bursting into tears or following it with a volley of punches.

Samantha closed the book and finished her mug of coffee. She got up to go to the kitchen and pour another, contemplating this latest step. "I don't think I can do this. Forgive Ben? He did the unforgivable. This writer is asking a lot from me. This is too extreme."

Just then the phone rang. "Hi Samantha. It's Mom."

"Mom? What's wrong? Is everyone okay?" Samantha was surprised to receive a call from her mother who never called her. She believed her mother was under the impression that her mother's phone only received calls and was incapable of making outgoing calls.

"Nothing's wrong, Samantha." Her mother never used the familiar Sam her father always called her by. Georgia was never George and Frances was never Frank. Her father chose the girls' names to replace the boys' names this family wouldn't produce. Samantha knew her mother hated these names and the bullying her father exerted in naming her and her sisters.

"What's up?" Samantha's suspicions were roused. The "nothing's wrong" did not mean that her mother lacked an agenda for this call

"Not much, Samantha. I was just sitting here with Frances and we were thinking of you."
Yeah, right you were thinking of me. Probably dissecting my current situation. Frances must be loving this.

"That's nice, Mom. How's Frances?"

"Fine dear. You know that William just got a promotion and we're going out Saturday to celebrate. Want to join us?"

Oh sure I want to join them. Two hours in a car to spend an evening with my dysfunctional family. How do I get out of this?

"Normally yes, Mom, but I have plans." Ah, the all allusive plans gambit. She actually wouldn't mind seeing her nephew Williams who managed to become a fully functioning adult, despite his mother's bitching and nagging at him. Samantha was always amazed that William never picked up a French chef knife and dispatched his mother. As a kid she often fantasized that fate for Frances.

"Well, suit yourself. Maybe sometime when the kids are with you we can have a visit. I haven't seen my grandchildren for so long." Whose fault is that? You can drive over here if you need to see them that badly.

"I don't suppose they're going to be with *Ben*," her mother continued, her voice rising with derision as she uttered Ben's name. " I don't want to interfere with your arrangements," right, Samantha thought, "but it seems he spends an awful lot of time with Edward and Cynthia."

"He's their father. He should be spending time with them. Quite honestly, I wish he spent more time with them."

"You don't mean *that*, Samantha. Don't you think he's, well, not the best role model for the children? Especially poor Edward?"

"Poor Edward? What about *poor* Edward?" Samantha felt her throat and stomach tighten as her mother stepped in where she had no business.

"He's at an impressionable age. Do you think he should be around a father who's a *philanderer*?"

Samantha wondered if her mother even knew what the word meant. Sounded like something Frances fed her. The purpose of the call was now clear - Ben bashing. Samantha wondered if her sister was on the extension.

"Mom, he's at an age where he needs his mother and father. Ben and I have worked hard to keep our personal problems away from the kids."

"Samantha, that's quite admirable. I mean your sisters and I all think you've been more than fair with Ben. But do you really think he **deserves** it?"

Just then the last chapter Samantha read clicked in her mind.

"Yes, Mom, I do. Say hi to Frances and Georgia for me. Bye."

Samantha hung up the phone, unconcerned about her mother's current feelings and opinions. She knew her mother and sisters had nothing better to do than kvetch and complain. The current topic had to be Samantha's failed marriage.

After a few deep breaths, long sips of coffee and a hard stare at the phone, Samantha picked up the receiver and dialed.

"Hi, Ben. It's Sam. Were you planning on going to the football game Friday to watch Edward and the band? Great - I'll see you there."

Samantha was on the road to forgiveness.

Chapter Six

Samantha woke in the near dark. Her fuzzy

mind realized that today was Friday...Friday night

football...Friday night seeing Ben. Oh goody.

Her feet touched the floor and her body followed

in a graceful bend. The calf muscles were stretching

nicely. She started jogging in place to Billy Joel's "My

Life" playing on the clock radio. A few days ago she

decided to switch stations from the depressing middle

East news of NPR to bouncy cheery classic rock. The

most news worthy event reported on that station was

where the local DJs were appearing to hand out free T

shirts.

Friday during football season meant extra

morning preparations. Sometimes the kids needed to

take extra clothes to school in case they were not

coming home before the game. Edward would need his

band uniform and instrument for a long distance away

game. Cynthia sometimes chose to go out with her

friends after school, grab a bite at the local Wendy's and then head back to school for the game.

At other times, usually home games, Cynthia deigned to come home with her brother who had to eat an early dinner, dress in his band uniform, and head over to the school. Cynthia would eat with them and go with her brother where she and her friends would decorate the student section with signs aimed to attract the attention of local sportscasters covering the game.

Samantha enjoyed the hectic Friday nights of getting everyone ready to go out and spend a few hours in what was becoming the bitter cold of autumn. She herself would layer on clothes and stay to watch the game. She would always stand at the fence to watch, too distracted by the constant chatter of the adults in the stand. Samantha never understood why they came. The men were too busy talking about their businesses and practices to pay attention; the women were too busy dishing out the local gossip. No one seemed to pay attention to the game until the student section would begin roaring with joy or dismay.

The kids were up, dressed, fed and ready to leave when Samantha came downstairs. She almost

never saw them get ready on their own, unless it was
Christmas morning and they were anxious to start the
gift unwrapping. In recent years they had even learned
to brew coffee and put out plates of cookies before
Samantha and Ben came downstairs. Why the sudden
burst of cooperation?

"When we saw Dad last night he said he would
be at the game tonight." Mystery solved. "We invited
him over for sloppy joes before we left. Okay?" Cynthia
and Edward both gave their sincerest imploring look.

"I suppose so. Just next time give me a heads
up before you issue invites. Does he know what time?"

"I told him we always eat by 5 so that Edward
can get dressed and leave on time." Cynthia was the
apparent inviter to this dinner. "He said he'd call you
today to let you know if he was coming."

"Fine. Now let's get going before we're all late."

Samantha gathered the breakfast dishes and
took them to the sink. She would need some self
therapy after dropping off the kids. She wasn't sure she
had the intestinal fortitude to deal with a family dinner
with Ben.

Another trip to the book - maybe there would be
help.

STEP THREE - FIND THE HUMOR

Self deprecation often leads to enlightenment

and enlightenment leads to self worth and

personal dignity

Lately, everyone want to tell me lawyer jokes.

Clients, friends, family, people I've just

met - they all want to share the latest vicious, but

humorous, assault on my profession. Usually, people are

polite enough to ask if I mind that they tell me their joke.

A doctor I was speaking to for the first time the other day

asked if I minded. I listened to him relate a joke I

previously heard and repeated to several other attorneys.

I then volleyed back with a quick one. "What's the

appropriate weight for a lawyer? Three and a half

pounds, and that includes the urn." I could tell another

twenty without missing a beat. Since you're curious,

here are some of the punch lines: "Professional

courtesy." "A good start." "Shoot the lawyer twice to make sure he's dead."

Why do I love lawyer jokes? Am I masochistic by nature? Well, in the first place, some of them are clever and funny. Secondly, I usually beat others to the punch by telling the hottest joke first so that they are deprived of what's become a Constitutional right to mock the legal profession. And third, I don't like taking myself so seriously that I would never think to make fun of myself for what I do for a living.

"And fourth," Samantha thought, "lawyers really *really* are assholes. I couldn't stand half of the partners Ben practiced with. Pompous, egotistical, arrogant *assholes.*"

How many of us are willing to own up to our foibles and peccadilloes? How many of us are willing to own up to our foibles and peccadilloes and joke about them? How many of us are willing to own up to our foibles and peccadilloes, joke about them and laugh out loud at ourselves? Are our numbers diminishing with each added clause?

I know people who would never admit to an imperfection or mistake, even when proof positive is staring them in the face or sitting on their heads. (That's a toupee or combover comment for those who can't admit to bad hair). "One blue, one brown sock - it's a fashion statement. Of course I know they're mismatched." "Seventy-five in a forty mile per hour zone? Your radar machine is off, Officer." "Of course I took a left when your directions said right - I wanted to take the scenic route." Sound familiar? Sound like you?

"Sounds like most of my family and especially Ben. They're never wrong."

You've got to own up to the fact that maybe, just maybe, you've made something of a mistake in some stage of your relationship with your spouse. Perhaps the mistake occurred in marrying this person in the first place. Perhaps you slipped up during the marriage and that slip up has led you this divorce. As stated in Steps

One and Two, you are not all knowing and controlling and neither is your spouse. You both bear some responsibility for the problems that led to the demise of your marriage. I have yet to meet the person who would qualify as the "innocent and injured spouse" required to obtain a divorce in some states. You both knew the buttons to push to put the other into a state of agitation and chances are neither of you hesitated to push them. Unless you are eligible for sainthood, you were a part, however small, of the problem.

"Whoa, whoa, whoa there. Okay, I may not be perfect. But this is on him. I really *am* the innocent and injured spouse." Samantha was not happy with this last tidbit.

What's this got to do with self-deprecation? The first step to really outstanding self-deprecation is to admit to some flaw, some mistake, some quirk that you can confess to the public. This does **not** mean, however, that you go to the extreme of self-flagellation that leads to an inability to forgive oneself as discussed in Chapter One.

All you have to do is admit you

are not perfect. You should still love yourself,

imperfections and all, but admit to and own your

mistakes.

Now that you can admit that there were

mistakes, try and find the humor in them. This may

even be automatic since many people make these sorts of

admissions only in a joking manner, unless they prefer

the ashes and sackcloth route. Rueful remarks and

sarcasm are welcomed here, again, as long as they don't

lead to self-flagellation. We're being playful with

ourselves, not hurtful. This is **constructive**, not

destructive, self-deprecation.

I really can't tell you how to do this since most

people do it instinctively in their own styles. Maybe

you're not comfortable with poking fun at yourself.

Maybe you've been the butt of too many jokes in your

lifetime to poke fun at yourself. The point is not in

making the comedy club circuit or in trying to become

the next Great American Humorist. The point is to not

take everything so deadly seriously.

This is tough, just like all the steps in this book.

But we all know that in addition to bringing some

measure of enlightenment, humor also relieves stress. If

you've never been severely stressed before, look out

because you're in for the Mother Lode. This is the

capital **S** stress, the kind that leads to eating disorders,

sleeping disorders, thinking disorders, disorders

disorders. This is the biggie. Along with the death of a

close family member, divorce is among the most stressful

life events we can experience. And we go through it in

the same manner as when we mourn the death of a

loved one with denial, anger, bargaining, depression and

acceptance.

Several years ago a close friend of mine lost his

father. Being of good Irish ancestry, David decided that

the way to deal with his father's death was to host a small

wake. My sister and I went to his apartment, drank heartily and told stories about Dave's dad. Since I didn't know this man well, I listened to David's stories ranging from his perceptions of his father when David was a small child to his most recent visits with his dad. We laughed hysterically throughout the evening. At the end, David hugged and thanked us for being with him and letting him enjoy memories of his dad.

I remembered that evening and made David promise that when my father passed away we would do the same. And so the weekend after my father's death, I headed back to New Jersey and met with David, my brother Alan and his wife Marie, and their best friends Bob and Lucille. We ate, drank and told Dad stories. I don't remember ever being so hung-over or laughing so much in recent years.

I still cry at times thinking about Dad, but without the cathartic opportunity to laugh with others over our more ridiculous and funny memories of him, I don't believe I would have progressed in my mourning as far and as fast as I did. I was able to remember my father as someone who loved a good joke, especially a good practical joke, and who loved me as well.

"Don't think about Dad, don't think about Dad, don't think about Dad. Too late," Samantha thought as some tears started rolling down. He's been gone for four years now; I should be over this by now.

At times throughout our marriages, we've shared a laugh (I hope) with our spouses, be it at each other, at some situation, or at a third party. We share inside jokes and code phrases that hold meaning only for two people who've shared intimacy and love. Try an remember those times. Remember the times when the two of you did something ridiculous or outrageous. Especially remember the times when your spouse went brain dead and did something ridiculous or outrageous. Remember the times when circumstances sent you into fits and spasms of laughter. Remember the good times.

Divorce with Dignity
Kathleen Berge Entenmann

Samantha thought of her love for Dudley Moore (Arthur) and John Gielgud (Hobbes) in "Arthur." One of her favorite scenes is when Arthur announces to a totally disinterested Hobbes that he is going to take a bath. "I'll alert the media," Hobbes replies. After that, all mundane announcements by either Samantha or Ben were met with the retort "I'll alert the media."

Ben preferred Bill Murray's humor and would randomly quote any line from "Caddy Shack." "I've got some stuff on order." "The Cinderella kid." "License to kill gophers by the government of the United Nations." "So I've got that going for me, which is nice." These lines were often recited, especially during a golf round.

Sunday funnies and daily comics routinely made their way to the refrigerator. One that always made Samantha smile was an old Calvin and Hobbes comic where Calvin is expounding on his love of turning nouns into verbs. "Verbing weirds language."

She thought about the time that she and the kids ganged up on Ben over the word "deja vu." One night at dinner, Edward innocently asked his father what "deja vu" meant and how to spell it. Always ready to expound on what he knew, Ben defined the word as "that funny feeling you've done something before." He then spelled it out. Five minutes later, Edward again asked how to spell "deja vu." Ben patiently obliged. A few minutes after that, Edward again asked for the spelling. Ben again obliged. The fourth time, Cynthia and Samantha could barely suppress the giggles as Edward asked the question. Finally, Ben realized he had been had and laughed at the clever joke his family played on him. Asking the spelling of "deja vu" always elicits a laugh from the family. Good times.

Samantha started laughing, thinking about all these bits and pieces of family humor. She began to feel better about dinner that evening and continuing with the book right now.

You'll especially need to remember these times when called upon to work with and cooperate with your spouse, whether finalizing an agreement or parenting your children. You need to remember the person who laughed with you and shared a private joke about the in-laws, out-laws and the children. You need that humor to smooth your ruffled feathers when you can't abide the thought of dealing with your spouse, your attorney, the courts, the kids, your friends, your family, the world.

Everyone you know will want a piece of you during this

process and you're going to need every ounce of courage

and humor in you to keep from biting off all their heads.

Not much that happens from here on in is going

to be funny to anyone, no matter how wacky a sense of

humor you have. You will be telling your most intimate

secrets to a total stranger (your new attorney) whom you

hope will get you what you think you deserve. If you're

going to trust this individual with your most important

private stuff, then by all means, find someone not hell

bent on plunging you into a greater depression than

you're already in. Try and find someone who is not a

clown but can help you see the lighter side of life

through this. Find someone who can help you see the

humor while still being professional. See Step Seven.

If this matter is litigated, you will be subjected to

probing questions from some total stranger who has

discussed your marriage, your sins, your faults, your

income, your entire personal history with your spouse.

You will be herded into and out of places you never

wanted to be - halls line with depressed, frustrated and

angry people who look ready for a fight with anyone who

dares to make eye contact. You will be judged for how

much you earn for a living as well as for what you don't;

for how well you parent as well as for how well you don't;

for the values you hold dear as well as for the values you

don't. And while marital misconduct does not play a

role in divorces in states with a no-fault statute, you will

be judged, however subliminally, on what part any

misconduct by you caused this dissolution of your

marriage and the current unhappy state of affairs.

Sound depressing? It is. I have yet to travel

through the Family Division or "Love Land" as attorneys

euphemistically refer to this unhappiest of all divisions,

without finding myself or my client shuddering. Even

with all my years of wandering those halls and appearing

before the various levels of justice lurking around every

corner, I don't presume to be able to place myself in the

emotional and mental position of all those litigants who

are waiting and waiting and waiting and waiting in those

halls to be called before a Domestic Relations Officer,

Hearing Officer or God forbid, an actual JUDGE!

Any truthful attorney will tell you the same. Not

only would they rather be elsewhere professionally, but

they cannot personally imagine the pain their clients

experience. For clients and litigants it is a mind numbing

experience you would rather trade for a root canal or

several hours of intense labor. At least after those

experiences you have a healthy gum and teeth or a little

bundle of joy. The frustration of the Family Division is

that oftentimes matters do not reach a final conclusion

without multiple visits and multiples dollars.

**"Oh joy, Ben and his friends were right. They're
gloating that family work is the worst seems totally
justified. I'm screwed!"**

But while you're in the midst of this sea of

despairing humanity, it truly helps if you can find

something humorous, be it in the irony of your fate or some sarcastic insight. This humor may help you cope with the situation. And if you are humor challenged or impaired, bring along some fun reading that tickles your funny bone. Now is not the time for gothic or Russian novels or non-fiction about the dismal fate of the world. Don't succumb to the sea of despair. Ride above those waves of depression until you leave that hell hole and reach safe harbor outside.

Tasks for Step Three

1. Make a list of the lighter moments that occurred during your marriage. Think of outrageous in-laws (or soon to be out-laws), family gatherings that were disasters, moments when you and your spouse acted like fruitcakes, clowns, nuts (choose your favorite metaphor). Commit these to memory.

"This will be a good time. I'm game." Samantha took out the journal she had begun keeping to record all her impressions about this time.

Fun times with Ben

Divorce with Dignity
Kathleen Berge Entenmann

1. The proposal at the beach. Sand everywhere and Ben trying to keep the sand from blowing on us.

2. The wedding. Ben's niece crying for "Uncle Ben" to pick her up and carry her down the aisle.

3. The time we nearly burned the house down lighting the new fireplace.

4. The Christmas when his younger brother decided to tell everyone he was gay at the dinner table and Hilda damn near had a stroke.

5. Deja vu.

6. Taking turns standing outside the kids' bedroom at the old house and shaking bells.

7. Seeing "The Producers." Nearly split a gut

over "Springtime for Hitler."

Bring on dinner tonight. I can handle any

drama.

Samantha closed her journal, put on her jacket and
headed out the door.

Chapter Seven

Samantha awoke in the near dark. She sprung out of bed and started her morning exercises before the radio even started. For a change she felt energetic and clear minded. Dinner with Ben last night reminded her of the times only a few months ago when she and Ben sat down to dinner with the kids. After some initial awkwardness, everyone began conversing like old times, sharing their adventures from the day, commenting on their personal concerns. Cynthia brought up the latest insanity at school; Edward brought up the latest crisis in the band room. Ben sat there bemused by the small talk he now missed on a nightly basis. Samantha kept serving the sloppy joes, giving everyone the occasional time check, making sure Edward would be on time for roll call before the game.

Once again the kids were fed and ready for school before Samantha reached the kitchen. Their smiles were painful reminders that last night meant so much to them. Samantha didn't know if they could withstand the heartache of their father not appearing at the dinner table on a regular basis. Ben made it clear to Samantha that his intentions were not to move back; he felt trapped by the kids' invitation to dinner and didn't want to say "no." He hoped Samantha would play the heavy and make it clear their father was not returning home.

The trip to school was full of talk about the game. Fortunately, neither Cynthia nor Edward pressed Samantha with questions about any possible reconciliation. Samantha hoped that Ben would man up over the weekend when he saw the kids and let them know he had no intention of returning home.

When Samantha got home, the phone was ringing. "Hello," she answered, hoping a telemarketer was not on the other end. Worse - it was her mother.

"Samantha, how are you?" Oh my God, there must be some catastrophe. Two phone calls from her mother in as many weeks. There must be a rip in the fabric of time and the universe is out of kilter.

"Fine, Mom. What's up?"

"Just wanted to see how you're doing. Anything new with Ben?"

"Yes, Mom. He came over for dinner last night before the football game. The kids invited him."

"And you let him come to the house? Do you really think that's such a great idea?"

Samantha had an overwhelming urge to hang up the phone and call Frances. She made the mistake of telling Frances yesterday that Ben would be coming over for dinner. Since Samantha ignored Frances's advice to not allow Ben in, she apparently told their mother what Samantha was up to. Up to? She was only placating her children by having their father over for a hurried meal of sloppy joes before a football game. She wasn't up to anything. But that's not how her mother would view this.

"Mom, you know I don't have a problem with Ben having access to the children. I don't know why you question this."

"Samantha, as usual you're missing the bigger picture. If Ben wants to see the kids after what *he's* done, don't you think you should use this to your advantage?"

"What advantage, Mom? I'm just happy he wants to spend time with them so that I can have a little me time."

"Samantha, have you spoken with your lawyer about this? Don't you think that you should use this as a bargaining chip? Let that adulterous s.o.b. pay for his sins."

"Mom, I'm going to do both of us a favor and end this. Goodbye."

Samantha honestly thought about pouring a Dewars. It wasn't even ten in the morning and her mother already had her on the brink of a nervous breakdown. The nerve of that woman. And the nerve of Frances. Samantha made a mental note never, *never* to discuss her personal life with her sisters. They were obvious conduits to her mother whose views were often diametrically opposed to Samantha's.

Soon doubt began to creep into Samantha's mind as she considered her mother's suggestion. Was it reasonable to make Ben pay for what he had done. But using the kids?

Time to turn to the book.

STEP FOUR - DON'T TAKE HOSTAGES

Using hostages displays your inherent weakness, rather than strength

The Iranian hostage crisis was a sad chapter of American history that occurred when I was in law school. Pictures of the blindfolded captive Americans flooded the news. Their fanatic Iranian captors coerced statements from their hostages who were obviously not having the time of their lives. These captors thought by doing this they were showing the world how they could bring the powerful United States, that great western devil, to its knees. These fanatics thought they could do this by capturing and torturing innocent victims.

Were these fanatics powerful? Of course not. Would the Soviet Union at that time have employed such a tactic against the United States in order to show its disagreements with us or our culture on the world stage?

Of course not. The Soviet Union had real power,

economic, military, nuclear and political and could face

an opponent on a level playing field. The Iranians,

lacking such resources, created power through the use of

threats to injure or kill all the innocent American

hostages, knowing that the United States does not

abandon its citizens in foreign lands who are threatened

by terrorists.

Think of every hostage situation you've ever

read about or witnessed on the evening news. How

powerful are these people who hold hostages in banks,

offices, or college campuses.

Without their guns or instruments of mayhem, not at all.

Since they have no legitimate power, they seize power

through whatever means available in order to steal,

intimidate or politicize. Afterwards when the crisis

finally passes through either negotiation or violence, they

are thought of as reprehensible and amoral cowards.

Divorce with Dignity
Kathleen Berge Entenmann

None of us applauds the terrorist who holds innocent lives hostage in order to obtain bargaining leverage. We reviled the Iranians during and after the hostage crisis and remain extremely wary of its government. It is unlikely that those of us who witnessed the hostage crisis, the death of the brave servicemen who attempted to rescue them, and the posturing of the Iranians, will be able to heal the psychic wounds left by this episode. We continue to have difficulty as a nation in reaching peaceful accords with a nation we regard as terroristic playground bullies. We have difficulty as a nation in forgiving those who create power imbalances through terror.

Power imbalances are tricky things; they can easily fluctuate back and forth, especially when one side seizes power through hostage taking. Iran held this country hostage as we each prayed daily for the end of the crisis and the safe return of our countrymen and women. But once the crisis was over, Iran found itself in the same power imbalance as before, and maybe in worse shape. Iran was able to hold center stage for months, but in the end, we took our money and our power, as well as the good will of the western world and once more left Iran in the cold.

We all experience power imbalances in our relationships and negotiations. I have been in situations where the playing field was not just uneven, it felt as though I was on the sinking half of the Titanic as it broke, rose and dove into the sea. I know the feeling of desperation as you're looking for that one extra chip, that one piece of leverage that will improve your lot or maybe carry the day. The temptation is to grab whatever you can to turn the table and win the day.

Oftentimes, that temptation is to take hostages. In s divorce, the choices are several and come in all shapes, sizes and ages. They include your children, your friends, your family, your pets and even your spouse. We don't need to brandish AK47s or nuclear weapons; we use our words and emotions. We play head games. We engage in emotional or financial extortion to get what we want.

The most common hostage victims are the children. I can't count how many times a distraught woman has related to me the following threat from her husband: "If you sue me for child support, I will take away custody of the children. You'll never see them again." Or slight variation to the last sentence: "You'll be the one with partial custody or visitation."

The reverse is where the custodial parent, usually the wife, threatens, "If you don't pay me what I want for support, you'll never see your children again." For a little added flair, the following "No judge in his right mind will give you any custody if you're not supporting your kids," adds some apparent gravity.

Now it's time for a reality check. For the distraught mother, I begin by asking who is the primary caregiver for the children. In the majority of cases, she's the one. In some rare instances, after careful cross-examination, I find that some form of co-parenting is the norm for this family. The reason these are rare instances is because the couple that has always co-parented is usually a couple that would not resort to threats. But where co-parenting is not the case, I find that Mom has been a fully functioning parent and Dad doesn't even know the kids' birthdays, much less their pediatricians, dentists, or teachers. This Dad is not going to get sole legal and physical custody.

So why the threat? This Dad knows that the children are this Mom's life. She has invested her energy, her creativity, and her resources in nurturing these children. She could accept any fate other than losing them. And Dad knows this all too well.

The threat of losing custody is Nonsense Threat 1a and I tell my clients as much. Often this requires a great deal of sympathetic listening and reassurance on my part that if Mom is being truthful about the children and the respective roles each parent has played, there is

no way she will lose custody of the children. I never

cease to be amazed at how the most intelligent and

emotionally strong women are blown away by this threat.

Of course Nonsense Threat 1B is telling the

distraught Dad he will never see his children unless he

pays a ransom in support. Somehow the added zinger

that no judge in his right mind would allow him to have

any custody adds authority to the threat, making Dad all

the more upset.

After careful examination, I learn the role Dad has

played in his children's lives. Generally those Dads who

are most concerned about this threat have played a

significant role in their children's lives. If they weren't

necessarily involved in the day to day details of clothing,

feeding, tutoring and medicating, they played major roles

in playing with them, joining in activities and spending

considerable time with them on weekends or during free

time from work. I assure them that at least in

Pennsylvania, our courts have yet to connect child

support with custody time.

What is accomplished by making these threats?

What is accomplished by trying to hold your spouse an

emotional hostage? Nothing. In fact, these threats will

be quickly dispelled by a competent attorney so that once

the initial fears are allayed, anger and a desire for

revenge take over. What could have been peacefully

negotiated turns into hardball negotiations. If you're

going to come after someone with a threat, make sure it's

one you can follow through on and take your best shot.

Don't write a check with your mouth that you can't cash.

If you're going to come after someone with this

sort of emotional extortion, you're only pouring kerosene

on a lit fire and creating the potential for a major

conflagration. Can you survive the ensuing holocaust?

Are you willing to risk months, perhaps years of

protracted litigation? Are you so sure that your threats

will put to a swift end what seems like endless litigation

that you are willing to risk total alienation with your ex-spouse? Do you have sufficient hair on your posterior to make this bet? If you think the answer is yes, read on for the likely consequences if you bet the wrong horse.

Consequence One: Other than holding the spouse's emotions in the above scenarios, the terrorist has also held the children hostage. For those who believe that the children can be completely shielded from this conduct and will never learn of the threats made to their father or mother, think again. Kids know everything that's going on, both from the loud or soft voiced verbal communications to the silent communications communicated by facial expressions and body language. As much as everyone proclaims and applauds the lofty ambition to keep the children out of this mess, they are always the unwilling participants.

Children fear and believe the absolute worst when change arrives. And when a parent is under attack, their sense of security is completely undermined.

Divorce with Dignity
Kathleen Berge Entenmann

They don't know who to turn to for comfort and support
- the seemingly strong parent attacking the weaker
parent or the parent who has always been their comfort
and strength. They are our hostages.

Because children are so easily targeted at a time
when they are most vulnerable, this is the issue I try to
resolve first - custody. This may be somewhat
counterintuitive because I'm trying to resolve the most
emotional issue at a time when people are their most
emotional. Why not wait until tempers have calmed and
rational discourse can prevail?

The reason for an early resolution is because
children deserve better than to have to wait until their
feuding parents stop acting like, take your pick,
hormonal adolescents, lobotomized fools, the Hatfields
and McCoys, or just plain jackasses. Children deserve to
be parented and loved and not become pawns in
negotiations that trade a parent's custodial time for either
material or financial gain. And while I hold absolutely

no illusions that during this initial time of stress and

depression that children are parented as they should be,

they will be parented much more effectively if their fate

is not sitting on an emotional seesaw while their parents

play out the passion play known as their divorce. It's just

not fair.

Even if you cannot arrive at a long term custody

agreement, remove the hostage situation by at least

agreeing to an interim arrangement that can be modified

at a later date when everyone's life is more settled.

Custody is seldom written in stone, unless in your

jurisdiction judges are reluctant to review custody unless

there is a catastrophic change as opposed to the standard

significant change of circumstances. And interim orders

or agreements labeled as interim are honored as such.

They're a temporary solution to an ongoing issue that

may need to be addressed or litigated in the future.

With the exception of sociopaths and

psychopaths who commit infanticide or other atrocities

on their children, all parents love their children. All

parents want what is in the "best interests of the

children," a truly nebulous meaningless standard. Why

so meaningless? Everyone wants what's in the best

interests of the children. The problem is agreeing on

what that is. Do you have the children raised by the

wealthier parent with more material goods but less

emotional and mental nourishment? Or the reverse? A

father's gruff and authoritarian manner can be viewed

by another as emotional abuse. A mother's easy going

discipline can be viewed by another as neglect. Whose

standard do you want to use? A newly elected judge

who's never decided these cases? In my mind, I can

parent your children better than you and in your mind,

you can parent mine better than me.

An appeal to the higher instincts of parenting is

not emotional blackmail if done with the sincere desire

to remove what can be a volatile issue by either a long

term resolution or a back burner solution. If your

bottom line is that you don't want to see your children suffer any more than they already are, don't be reluctant to bring some closure to the children's issues. If your motives are to use the children as human shields, then you probably weren't paying attention during the introduction when I advised you not to buy this book.

If you have not been the primary caregiver for your children, please be honest with yourself and your intentions concerning custody. You may think you want "100% custody" whatever that is when what you really want is to spend more time with your children. If that's the case, don't be dishonest with your demands and intentions. This is not an open air market where people make outrageously high demands which are met with outrageously low offers, only to meet somewhere in the middle. Your demand for sole or primary custody as a bargaining chip in order to obtain more that an every other weekend or few evenings each week custody is wrong. This strategy can backfire on you when your bluff is called and everyone, especially your now distraught spouse, realizes that you were bluffing. If that happens, not only have you tried to turn your spouse and children hostages, you've blindfolded yourself and turned yourself into another hostage.

Consequence Two: Yes, you can hold yourself hostage in this divorce as well. It's similar to the case of the paranoid homeowner who decides to keep a loaded handgun in the nightstand. When the burglar breaks into the house, the inexperienced gun-wielding homeowner, brandishing his never before fired gun quickly becomes the hostage of the smarter, faster and criminally intentioned thief. The criminal now extends his activities beyond mere stealing to terror and mayhem. Lesson? When you can't follow through on your threats, your spouse exposes you as the paper tiger you are and turns the situation around. You are now the hostage. You have lot any power or credibility you had. Not a pretty picture.

Divorce with Dignity
Kathleen Berge Entenmann

Additionally, your spouse's attorney will now be encouraged by a seriously peeved client to engage in a legal form of mortal combat. Your spouse now wants to make sure your life is a living hell and that you will spend as little time as possible with your children. Negotiations over the simplest of issues will require the skill and perseverance of a gladiator to get past the refusals by your spouse to deal with someone who makes outrageous and unsupportable demands. You will now incur incredible attorney fees as your attorney goes to combat over issues that a calmer you, without the threats, could have negotiated face to face with your spouse over the kitchen table.

All of us at one time or another have suffered the indignity of shooting ourselves in the foot. Sometimes it's a gamble with minor consequences, a bluff during a sales negotiation that didn't pan out, a practical joke that backfired with not so funny results. This isn't the time to bet that your scheme with work without negative consequences. The stakes are way too high for that. You may set into motion not only custody problems and litigation that will continue throughout your children's minority, but set back progress on property and other economic settlements. The stakes also involve your mental and emotional stability during a particularly stressful time in your life. Again, do you have that kind of nerve and can you afford any negative results?

Consequence Three: The other people who are held hostage in this divorce are those who care deeply enough about you to take an interest in and listen to your problems. They may include parents, siblings, relatives, friends and coworkers, as well as that interesting category, *significant others*. Depending on their closeness to you and their involvement with your problems, they become your witting or unwitting hostages as you emotionally blackmail them as well. How?

Divorce with Dignity
Kathleen Berge Entenmann

Many of my clients left their parents' nest years before marriage, working or attending school, seldom returning home except for holidays and an occasional meal. Others left the parental nest on the day of their weddings. Yet when my clients' marriages started to fall apart, no matter how independent or dependent they are on parental support, the first people they ran to for comfort and support were Mom and Dad. There's nothing wrong with this; as a mother I encourage my children to seek my support. Unfortunately, I think they think they're CIA operatives; they'd tell me what's going on, but then they'd have to kill me.

There's nothing wrong with seeking comfort from Mom and Dad unless every decision that must be made in this divorce is thrust upon them. "I'm too upset; I don't know what to do. You decide for me." I wonder how many of these people were able to survive the years of marriage prior to this divorce without constant parental intervention. I get a glimpse into what may have been a significant contributing factor to the divorce - an inability to deal with life without constant parental approval and consent.

Thrusting this problem on Mom and Dad to solve is thrusting them into the eye of your emotional hurricane. As soon as they break out of the hurricane to resolve the problem and interject themselves into your divorce, they will be rebuffed by your spouse, both attorneys and maybe even you. Mom and Dad can't win, but they'll go ahead and intervene because that's what parents do and that's what we expect from them. They have become your hostages. They hope that by doing the right thing by you they will have restored your emotional equilibrium and all will be right with the world.

Overly relying on anyone, not just Mom and Dad, but Sister, Brother, Friend, Significant Other and Adult Children can be a hostage taking situation. Don't do it; in the end, all hostages learn to despise their captors and these people will be no different. Remember that some of these people, especially your adult children, have an equally close relationship with your spouse. You're now asking them to take sides, to alienate a close friend, parent or in-law.

Don't ask for money from these people, unless it's a last resort. At some point you have to learn to become self-sufficient. Also don't insist on solutions to problems. Use your supporters as a sounding board, but take responsibility for your own choices. You'll gain strength and self-respect and preserve these cherished relationships.

For both spouses: The hostage checklist

1. Am I making a reasonable demand or am I threatening my spouse?

2. Can I back up my demand with action, if necessary, or am I full of hot air?

3. Will my children resent my actions later on in life (more than they normally would)?

4. Am I seeking advice or seeking someone to take on my problems for me?

5. Will I respect myself tomorrow or a year from now for my conduct today?

Tasks for Step Four

1. Make a list of your demands for settling this divorce.

2. Review the list carefully, evaluating each and every demand according to this criteria:

a. Is it reasonable?

b. Does it make sense?

c. Am I entitled to this?

d. Will any third party (children, family, friends, spouse) be hurt by this?

e. Do I really even want this?

3. Now review your edited list (if any demands have been removed or modified). Ask yourself the following: Am I willing and able to do what is necessary to see that this demand becomes reality?

Samantha thought about her wish list of demands. She thought about where she wanted to be at the end of this. She thought about Ben and what was fair. Mainly she thought about the kids, the disruption to their lives, the need for some stability.

"Okay... here goes..."

Samantha put pen to paper and wrote the following:

1. Keep the house at least until the kids get through school.

2. Have enough money to pay the mortgage, pay for repairs, feed and clothe the kids and me.

3. Be able to afford to either go back to school or start a job. I don't expect to start at the top in a new career. I may need some additional schooling.

4. Keep all the furnishings.

5. A huge chunk of Ben's 40K.

6. At least half of the savings account.

7. See Ben publicly humiliated.

8. Get professional help – I may be nuts. I

want inner peace.

Samantha reviewed the list. She didn't include

custody because she thought that was a foregone

conclusion. Just in case Ben wanted to play games

there, she revised the list to add:

9. Primary custody of Cynthia and Edward

until they graduate high school. Ben to pay

all of their college expenses, even if they

choose one of the Ivys.

Samantha then reread her list. Other than Ben's

public humiliation and her inner peace, she didn't see

anything unreasonable. She had always been there for

the kids; they deserved to stay in their house. Too bad if

Ben wanted to sell it and split the proceeds; where was she going with the kids? They should stay in their school district with their friends. At least they both were still doing well in school.

She didn't know if she was on shaky ground with Ben's 401k. She thought her first lawyer mentioned that this was a marital asset and should be split. But how?

Support - who knew when she'd be able to support herself, much less the kids. She and Ben had to work out a fair number on this. So far the current support order for herself and the kids was adequate, but she heard occasional rumblings from Ben. He caused this, *he* caused this, ***he caused this!*** I don't care who's a hostage here; it's his fault. He should just man up and take care of his own family ***first.***

Samantha had to find a good lawyer. She would need one.

Chapter Eight

Samantha awoke in the near dark. She wondered whether today would be a repeat of recent school days where the kids jumped out of bed, got themselves dressed and even made breakfast. She wondered but felt confident that they were back to Samantha's morning get ready plan. She hoped her morning shower and stretches were enough to prepare her for the conflict about to be staged in her home.

Samantha spoke with Ben yesterday before he left with the kids for his weekly night out of local restaurant food and perhaps a movie. She expressed her concern that the kids might be getting the wrong message from his recent dinners with the family. She expressed her concern that maybe she was getting the wrong message from his recent dinners with the family. Did he want to come home?

She now wished she had never started the questioning. After much hemming and hawing, and Ben's usual lawyer b.s., Ben told Samantha, in no uncertain terms, that as much as he loved his family and the feeling of being part of their lives, he simply wanted to move on. No, it was not someone special. Yes, he wanted to finalize the divorce.

During their dinner at Antonio's that evening, Ben did tell the kids that he never intended to come back home. He told them that it wasn't Mom's fault; he was the one who wanted a different life. He told them not to blame Samantha. He told them, but they didn't believe.

Cynthia was the first to come tromping into the house. "I hope you're happy," she screamed at a startled Samantha. "Dad doesn't want to come home. I know you said something to him to make him stay away." With that, Cynthia ran upstairs and slammed her bedroom door, sobbing loudly enough to startle the dogs.

Edward entered next, calmer than his sister. "Dad told us he doesn't want to come home. He said it's not your fault. Is that true?" At least her son was willing to ask questions instead of just hurling accusations.

"Yes, Edward. Your Dad wants a new life. He loves us but he doesn't want to live with us." Samantha started to tear up as she watched her son's posture sag as he dragged himself to his bedroom.

Divorce with Dignity
Kathleen Berge Entenmann

"Oh great," thought Samantha as she hit Ben's speed dial number. "Two depressed kids. Pick up, pick up, **pick up!**"

Ben was on his way to tonight's date, a paralegal from a friend's law firm. He heard the call, saw Samantha on the caller i.d., and chose not to answer. "Nothing good can come from this," he thought. "I'll talk to her tomorrow."

When Ben failed to answer, Samantha went up to the kids' rooms. Edward opened the door and Samantha gave him a huge hug. She then guided him over to Cynthia's room where a red eyed daughter met them. Samantha pulled both kids inside Cynthia's room, sat them on her bed while she cleaned off Cynthia's desk chair and sat down.

"Okay, what do you want to say?" Samantha calmly invited them to talk, to air out their grief.

Cynthia started with a torrent of words, her anger at both her parents filling the room. Why was this happening to her? Sure she knew other kids whose parents were divorced, but why was this happening to her? Sure she knew that Samantha was always there for her, but why was this happening to her? Why were her parents doing this *to her?*

Edward listened to his sister, his head bent down on his chest. When Cynthia stopped, he listened to his mother explain that this happens, it wasn't what she wanted, their father chose a new life over theirs. Yeah, it sucks. Yeah, it's depressing. But Mom and Dad would always be there for Cynthia and Edward and Mom would do her best not to have their lives disturbed any worse then they already were. Mom would keep them in school. Mom would keep them in their home. Mom would always be, well, Mom.

With that, Edward stood up from the bed, stepped over Cynthia's piled clothes, climbed into his mother's lap and hugged her. He then left the room and went into his own, got ready for bed and climbed under the blankets. He knew his mom would be in shortly to tuck him in, something she now only did when he was sick or upset.

As soon as Edward left, Cynthia blew her nose on the tissue her mother handed her and stood to hug Samantha. "I'm sorry, Mom. I just thought Dad was going to come back. I didn't mean what I said tonight. I know you're there for us. I love you."

With that, Samantha left her daughter's room, slipped into her son's to kiss him good night and returned to the living room. She stopped for a glass of wine on the way, turned on the classical station, and began to swear out loud. The swearing was not loud enough to be heard by the kids who were being lulled by the music. The swearing was under her breath and contained every oath she could think of about Ben. She successfully conjugated the f-bomb into several parts of speech with Ben as the object in all the sentences. She cried buckets of tears, more than she had since Ben left. She thought about her depressed children and took her depressed self to bed.

Now it was morning and time to face the emotional fallout. She stretched, showered and dressed, stopping at the kids' bedrooms on the way down. No one was in them. When she reached the kitchen, half-scared that they had run away from her during the night, she saw them seated at the table.

Samantha had prepared scrambled eggs and toast. A plate greeted Samantha at her seat.

It was then that Samantha knew they'd really be okay. They'd be okay, but she wouldn't bet on Ben's future. Forget the hostage chapter. This was war. She ate her breakfast with a smile on her face and homicide in her heart.

Cynthia and Edward seemed enthused to be going to school, shouting a cheerful "Have a great day, Mom," as they walked into the building. Thank God for His blessings, she thought. This was all her work, all her steadfastness, all her courage being rewarded by two grateful kids.

Unbelievable.

As Samantha started to pull away from the curb, she saw her friend Paula in the rear mirror. Samantha quickly put the car back into park, lowered her window, and waved to her friend. Paula pulled into the space behind Samantha, got out of her car and walked up to Samantha's open window.

"Hey, girlfriend. Long time no see." Paula opened with her usual greeting.

"What's new, what's happening?" Samantha replied.

"Not much. Want to go to Starbucks?"

"How about that new place next to the library - Nancy's?"

"Sure. See you there." With that both women pulled out and drove over to the town's latest coffee shop. Once the barista delivered the two pumpkin latte orders, the conversation began in earnest.

"Jordan told me she saw you about a month ago after your breakup with Ben. Sorry I haven't called, but you know..." Paula looked and sounded uncomfortable.

"It's okay. I've been a bit preoccupied and really didn't feel like company." Samantha wanted to break the awkwardness. She too felt uncomfortable and didn't want this feeling to permeate the reunion.

"So, how *are* you? The kids look fine."

"Yeah, everyone's doing fine. We've had some tussles, but overall, it's been better than I thought it would be." Samantha thought about last night's meltdown with the kids and how grateful she was that the kids seemed fine this morning.

"And Ben? Do you see him often?" Paula was hunting for the lowdown.

"He has the kids once or twice a week, depending on his schedule. He has them for most of the weekend every other week. Again, depends on his schedule."

"You guys ever talk?" A loaded question.

"Well, yes, for the most part. Last night I tried calling him after he dropped off the kids, but there was no answer."

"An emergency?"

"More of a melt down. The kids were having a hard time dealing with the divorce and something he said to them made them snap. I dealt with it, but I really wanted to talk to him about it and he wouldn't pick-up. I m-f'd him in absentia for several minutes after that."

"Well, I don't know why you haven't totally lost your cool with him. I always thought he lacked class. If it weren't for you he'd be some middle manager in some dead end job instead of a big-time lawyer. If it weren't for you..." and with that Paula was off to the races, trash talking Ben to pieces. She used some of her own curse words, adding a few that Samantha hadn't thought of.

She added her thoughts about what she considered to be reasonable punishment for Ben after the hell he put Samantha through. And she made sure that Samantha knew that all their friends supported Samantha and everyone had doubts about Ben.

After Paula's venting, the conversation turned to local topics of interest. Together they resolved the public education crisis in their own community (go ahead and build the much needed new high school) as well as education needs nationwide. Samantha knew that when she was made kingess, benevolent dictator of the world, Paula would be her Minister of Education and other Important Social Issues. Right.

When Samantha left Paula and reached home, she felt exhausted from the time spent with her friend. She put on a pot of coffee, not wanting the caffeine buzz to die, and settled down with the book. As usual and as uncanny as ever, the next step dealt with the most recent crisis she faced.

STEP FIVE: MINIMIZE THE DISRESPECT

Divorce with Dignity
Kathleen Berge Entenmann

How can you respect yourself when you sling

mud at others?

How many of us have had the following
conversation?

"So how's (fill in the name of your spouse)?"
friend/associate/family member asks.

"Well, we're separated right now. I'm going to
file for divorce..."

"You know, I never did like (spouse's name). I
knew he/she wasn't right for you. He/She always was
such a .... (choose one: cheap bastard, womanizing
worm, control freak, drunken bitch, etc.).

"Well, sad to say you were right. I've had such a
difficult time putting up with him/her. That so and so
really ticked me off for the last time. You know what
he/she did?"

And then the story continues on with a litany of
your spouse's faults, sins and acts of depravity so vile that
any judge with an ounce of common sense would grant

you a divorce on the spot. Not only would the divorce be granted, but you would receive **all** the assets, full custody of your children, and were it in the judge's power, throw your spouse in prison for life. Or so goes the fantasy.

It's so easy to play the game Slam the Spouse because this is human nature. We live in a society that thrives on getting its jollies at the expense of others. If you question that, just watch television for all the so-called reality programs that ridicule its participants. We also live in a society that plays the blame game when things go wrong. Many are never personally responsible when things go wrong. We either point a finger at someone else, or blame the ubiquitous "nobody" who always seems to be at the center of all mischief. Why should now be any different? Let's point the finger at our spouse. Let's make a bold statement about our lack of integrity by not accepting our role.

Another reason why bad mouthing our spouse is easy? This is entertainment for friends and family during your divorce. For the same reasons you and your

spouse are deciding to divorce are the same reasons why

your family an friend want to see you apart. For every

instance of marital misconduct you can list, your friends

and family can list ten others. It seems that very little of

your life together was truly private.

You thought your husband was a womanizer?

Wait until your best relates to you how your husband put

the moves on her at the pool parties. She never spoke up

until now because she didn't want to hurt your feelings

or put your marriage in jeopardy.

You think your wife had a drinking problem?

Wait until your sister tells you about her surprise visits to

your spouse in the middle of the day. Your wife was

totally loaded and slurred every syllable during their very

uncomfortable talk.

The bottom line is that no matter how well you

think you know your spouse, your friends and family

have revelations they kept from you. They honestly

believed they were doing you a favor. They also didn't want to get in the cross-fire by revealing their anecdotes and becoming the cause of your divorce. But now that you're getting divorced anyway, what the hell?

Some of us need to share the bad stories for the validation we receive when told that we're doing the right thing in divorcing this person who has so wronged us. But after we've opened our personal Pandora boxes and let out all the evil inside, others do the same. Sometimes this becomes a braggart's contest, everyone trying to one-up each other.

In all fairness, many of these people are just trying to be supportive and validate our feelings. In all seriousness, however, many are in this to witness a raging inferno and to add fuel to the fire. Watch whom you choose to confide in. The emotional support you seek may only be an opportunity for someone else to help script your personal soap opera for their own amusement.

Divorce with Dignity
Kathleen Berge Entenmann

This is dangerous ground for another reason -
kids. How can you co-parent with someone with whom
you view as the Grim Reaper of your happiness? How
do you effectively say to your children that they should
respect Mom/Dad when you publicly denounce this
person as a fiend or a slug or a fiendish slug? Either you
must be one helluva actor or schizophrenic to pull off
that dichotomy. Remember, kids know better than to
simply listen to what you tell them and they will deeply
resent you for dissing Mom/Dad. That bears repeating.
They will deeply resent you for dissing Mom/Dad.
They have enough pain, thank you, without you telling
them that one of the people they count on is not worthy
of their respect.

And please don't hide behind "I'm only telling
my kids the truth. I've raised them to be honest and they
need to hear this." Nonsense! Are you also raising your
children to be malicious and to inflict pain on others?
Because that's exactly what you're doing - inflicting

emotional pain on your children by telling them ugly

stuff about their other parent. And since when did you

become the ultimate arbiter of the truth? Who's to say

what's the truth and what's your distorted perception of

the truth during this time of intense emotional pain?

Can you be objective and separate fact from fiction when

discussing a person who's caused you a tremendous

amount of hurt, anger, anxiety, frustration and

depression? Bravo for you if you can. You're a rarity

and probably not in need of this book because you're a

candidate for sainthood.

"That's a little harsh. I remember the truth and
the truth is that Ben has ruined our lives. I'm no saint,
but I can separate fact from fiction." Samantha read on,
refusing to believe she was unfair in her Ben bashing.

When the temptation presents itself to really

unload on your spouse, remember the Spanish proverb

in the first step: ***Living well is the best revenge.***

Really living well also means living within a moral code

that forbids disclosing the personal problems of others

and showing disrespect to fellow human beings. Fellow human beings include spouses, both current and former, although sometimes their conduct makes it difficult to think of them as human beings.

If you *must* engage in this verbal attack for purposes of validation or emotional catharsis, I would recommend unloading on one of the following:

Your closest friend who has no ties to your spouse and who would never consider betraying your confidences to anyone. A truly close friend will listen to you babble endlessly, comfort your crying, permit you to crash on a couch when you're too exhausted to continue, make a pot of coffee in the morning, and listen some more to you. A truly close friend will not force judgements on you about your spouses's character, your situation, your decision making. A truly close friend probably will not offer advice, except to seek professional help, both legal and psychological. Most importantly, a truly close friend will not make the situation any worse than it already is by spreading your tales so that you can't show your face in public.

Remember also, that when you speak unflatteringly about your spouse, you also paint an unflattering picture of yourself. If your spouse was so bad, why didn't you end this sooner? Are you a masochist, a wimp, an idiot? A truly close friend will help you to continue to think well of yourself.

Your attorney on a one-time basis only.

Your attorney needs to know the details of your life that impact legal decisions concerning custody or economic issues. To the extent that the horror stories you have to tell about your spouse contribute to your attorney's ability to effectively represent you, they must be disclosed. However, once you've told your tale, don't repeatedly return to it. Believe me, your attorney has made extensive notes, both written and mental, of the legally significant facts of your living hell. By continually reliving your vivid memories of marital misconduct, or verbalizing your hopes for legal vindication, you do not

assist your attorney in representing you. You will be

advised that while these matters are unfortunate and you

have suffered great emotional harm, you will not receive

"justice" through the courts as payback for the

mistreatment you received.

This isn't to say that you completely ignore the

marital misconduct and the reasons why your spouse is a

louse, even in a no-fault jurisdiction. To the contrary,

more and more jurisdictions are getting into marital torts

arising from the conduct of one spouse to another.

Upon your attorney's advice, you may want to take legal

action against your spouse for outrageous and egregious

conduct. If your spouse treated you cruelly, both

physically and mentally, you should advise your attorney

as this conduct may be actionable apart from the issues

involved in the divorce itself.

Your priest, minister, rabbi or other

religious leader who has a duty of

confidentiality. In addition to their duties of

confidentiality, clergy can offer support, counseling and

guidance. You may want to consult and confide not only

to get this off your chest, but also to receive this support,

counseling and spiritual guidance to deal with the effects

this has had on you.

"Not gonna happen. So not gonna happen."

Samantha thought of her last encounter with Reverend

Dick. Since then she hasn't returned to that church.

A counselor or therapist who's helping

you work through this. In order to effectively deal

with the emotional and mental fallout, you will have to

be candid with these people. If you seek professional

help to deal with the pain of your separation or divorce,

feel free to unload about the other spouse. However, be

prepared to answer the question my mother would

always ask my sisters and me when we'd complain to her

about some act of sibling nastiness: And where were you

when all this was happening? You may have to confess

honestly to your role in provoking the actions you now complain of.

Speaking of mothers, please don't dump all your problems on Mom or Dad, sister or brother. Especially don't unload on your spouse's family members, no matter how sympathetic they may be. In the end, blood is thicker than water (cliche, but true) and your in-laws will become your outlaws because they don't want the guilt of having raised the monster you're portraying their child as. Even if you have a closer relationship with one of your spouse's siblings than that sibling has with your spouse, beware of the tension you're creating in that family. You may be starting a civil war within your in-laws. You will also want to maintain the good will of your children's grandparents, aunts, uncles and cousins on both sides who will continue to have a relationship with you through your children.

If you think your whining and complaining to your friends and family is for purposes of explaining this divorce, think again. First, your statements only raise

further questions: Well, if it was that bad, why did you

stay married for so long? Are you sure that he/she can't

be cured or reformed? Why won't you forgive him/her?

Let me go talk to him/her. Let me see if my gun's

loaded. I know a guy who knows a guy who can take

care of this ***permanently***.

Good way to bring everyone into the fray. While

you may be having fun watching your father and burly

brothers kick some serious butt, or your mother and

sisters verbally bitch slap, you're not getting through this

divorce with any measure of personal dignity. The

bottom line is that after they've kicked some serious butt

or bitch slapped, you're the one left to disentangle your

life from someone now thoroughly ticked off at you and

your family. Try negotiating with that person.

Furthermore, by going to your family with your whining,

you've confirmed their long held belief that you are

incapable of dealing with life by yourself without their intervention and assistance.

The second reaction by your friends and families is typified by the first question: Why did you stay married for so long? This question begs to bring out your martyr: For the kids. For appearances. For you, my friends and family, so I could shield you from my personal hell. Problem here?

First, your friends and family now think you're a fool for remaining with a person who is as abusive as you've portrayed. While we live in an age where we are all victims of some sort, we also live in an age where people are pretty sick and tired of hearing about someone else's victimization. At best we are entertained by others' victimization which explains the rash of reality shows where people air their complaints about others. It's okay for me to be a victim, just not okay for you.

As much as we don't like to openly admit this, women fall in rank on **both** sides of the victim issue, whether it's the tale of a bad marriage, bad employment or even criminal victimization such as rape. "Why did you put yourself in that position?" "Don't you know you've undermined the credibility of all women by subjecting yourself to that abuse?" And the ultimate judgement: "She had it coming to her." These reactions may be countered by those who offer sympathy and comfort. But the preceding negative comments, whether verbal or silent, are not uncommon reactions. These comments will not feed your need for positive feedback.

For men, your masculinity will be called into question. "You should have shown that bitch the door. Real men don't wallow in self-pity. What kind of man are you? You don't have to put up with that crap for anyone's sake." Make you feel warm inside? I don't think so.

This is why you go to your best friend, attorney, clergy or therapist. Even if these people have these reactions, their thoughts will go unexpressed as they put a comforting arm around you, assure you you're okay,

and offer help to see you through. Know that this person

won't repeat a word you've confided. The last thing you

need is for your spouse to hear about your complaints

through the grapevine and is ready to rumble.

The second reaction to the martyr routine is that

it's fairly easy for others to dismiss. No one believes

anyone is that self-sacrificing and no one likes to hang

out with a martyr. Your loved ones will resent your years

of sacrifice if the reason you give for putting up with

your spouse's marital misconduct is your concern for

their feelings and opinions. No one wants to bear the

burden of being the reason for someone else' martyrdom

or self sacrifice.

Your children especially don't want to hear

about your sacrifice for their sakes. I know a woman

who separated from her physically and emotionally

abusive husband when her children were preschoolers.

The couple met at a small bible college where she was a

practicing Christian and he was a practicing cretin. But

he charmed her, wed her and made babies with her.

Sometime after the wedding, his proclivities for

various forms of cruelty surfaced. She tolerated this

insanity until the youngest child was five "for the sake of

the children." But she finally reached her saturation

point and could stand no more. She left, with her

children, filed for support, found an entry level position,

and began supporting herself and her children on her

modest wages which have grown over the years.

Although a devout Christian who should turn

the other cheek, she found it difficult to remain silent

about her ordeal. By the way, this is not to suggest that

devout Christians should not react to abuse and simply

turn the other cheek. But the constant whining and

complaining in front of the children kept them aware

that their mother was desperately unhappy and their

father was the cause of that unhappiness. Unfortunately,

they also became aware that the only reason their mother endured this abuse was for their sake.

The rest of the story does not have a happy ending. The children were quickly sickened by lines such as "I'll be okay while you're out having fun with your father and his new girlfriend. Don't worry about me while I clean your rooms, wash your clothes, start your homework. I'll be fine by myself." Tired of Mom's unceasing martyrdom, the kids decided to move in with Dad.

They overlooked all his faults since he was now a whole lot more fun than Mom, showering them with attention and affection. They resented Mom's resentment of their close relationship with Dad. No one, including your children, likes a martyr.

Finally, once you've entered the public arena of viciously denouncing your spouse, you make future encounters difficult, if not impossible, Every zinger, every criticism, every negative comment now sets the agenda for future discussions between you and your

spouse. Even when the ink is dried on a marriage

settlement agreement or divorce decree, you will

continue to negotiate with this person on issues involving

your children, your family, your friends or your business

associates. Unless one of you becomes a cloistered nun

or Tibetan monk, move to the opposite coast or becomes

an ex-patriate, you will still have contact with each other.

Those contacts multiply by the number of children,

friends or organizations you share. Do you really want

everyone at your country club to know your personal

business? Do you want scathing or, worse yet, pitying

looks at church? Do you want unsolicited advice from all

you know?

Keeping your personal life personal is difficult in

an age of internet and personal social networking where

we're encouraged to share our feelings. Keeping your

personal life personal when the overwhelming

temptation is to spill out all the gore is incredibly tough.

So do yourself, your spouse, your children, your friends,

your family a favor - **_Don't!_**

"Easier said than done. It's too tempting.

Everyone wants to hear the dirt. I want to hear the dirt.

What idiotic tasks do I have to do now?" Samantha was

not happy about the advice to keep quiet.

Tasks for Step Five

1. Make a thorough list of all the negative things you

    would like to say about your spouse. Go for broke!

    Don't hold back! Express yourself!

2. Now follow the directions for the quiz at the

    beginning of the book. Trash your list.

    Samantha found one of Ben's half-used legal

pads and began writing.

1. *Ben's suffering from a middle age crisis*

   and is pathetic. The club, the clothes, the

   young bimbo.

2. *Ben is the most unfaithful person.*

3. I should have known something was wrong with him when I met his mother.

4. He's a worm.

5. He's arrogant. No one is good enough for him.

6. I hate what he did to the kids. I really do hate what he did to the kids.

7. He's a coward.

8. He's insecure about his masculinity.

9. Everything I said the other night – ditto.

Samantha looked at the list. It was far from exhaustive, but she ran out of energy. The list ended up in the trash. No more.

Chapter Nine

Samantha awoke in the near dark. She wanted to stay in bed and pull the covers over her head. Today was not a get up and get 'em kind of day. Today she dreaded. Today she would start visiting lawyers, a job she had delayed as long as possible. Oh well, got to face this sooner or later. "Later," her procrastinating self shouted in her head. "Shut up," Samantha replied out loud.

The school routine had become, well, routine. By now the kids were up by themselves unless they required a mental health day or an actual illness struck. She made arrangements for them to come home by themselves and filled the cookie jar with fresh Toll House cookies. No matter how old they aged, they still wanted cookies and milk after school.

Samantha showered and dressed, choosing one of her black and red sweaters and a great pair of black wool slacks. No heels for this outing; she knew she needed to be as comfortable as possible. She heard the stories about some of the distraught women who showed up at Ben's firm for a divorce consultation. She was not going out dressed like them in sweats and a message t-shirt. She'd try to appear confident and put together, totally belying her inner panic at the thought of talking to a stranger about her life. Root canal looked like a better option at this point.

As she left the house with the kids she grabbed the list of questions she wrote down last night after she had read the latest chapter about selecting an attorney. Samantha wanted to make sure she asked this attorney about all her concerns and wanted to make sure those concerns were addressed. She hoped the book's advice would help.

STEP SIX - DON'T HIRE A SHARK

Your choice of attorney is a personal reflection of your sense of self worth and personal dignity.

Don't hire a slime ball.

I respect the majority of attorneys I've had the privilege of practicing with and litigating against. However, the stories are legend in my local family division of attorneys who are not to be trusted, who seek an unfair advantage, and who purposely drive up the

cost of divorce through unnecessary paperwork,

unreasonable demands and/or incompetent lawyering.

These lawyers are labeled "sharks" because their hunger

for unfortunate victims, either their own clients or the

opposition, rivals their hunger of their predatory

namesakes. The destruction wrecked by their lawyering

practices spreads to their own clients, clients' spouses and

opposing counsel. Their destruction spreads like blood

in the water and only fuels their appetite for more pain

and expense.

My personal definition of a shark: A lawyer who

does not weigh the potential emotional and financial cost

when engaging in battle over any issue in a divorce. Any

issue includes custody, property and support. A shark

will tell a client that you must go after every last dime, or

conversely, protect every last penny. A shark will

misrepresent the legal fees it will cost you to go for every

dime or protect every penny until your legal bill exceeds

what you've received or protected. A shark will convince

you that this litigious course of conduct is worth the

money you're about to invest. A shark will drop you like

a bad habit the moment the legal fees are not paid. If a

shark doesn't drop you for non-payment, he/she will

wait until the end of property distribution and walk away

with the lion's share of your marital property in payment

of your outstanding fees. A shark will allow you, even

sometimes encourage you, to go through hell and back,

fighting your spouse tooth and nail, in order to satisfy

some sadistic need for *schadenfreude.*, pleasure at another's

misfortune.

Some clients think this is exactly what they want

from an attorney. Some clients think they want a tough

street fighter who will go to the wall for them and make

sure their spouse doesn't take advantage of them. The

problem is that they make it so easy for the shark to take

advantage of **them** by convincing the client they are

acting in the manner required by the circumstances.

Instead, these attorneys are acting in the manner required to enhance their personal fortunes.

While you may think you need a tough attorney, some bully who makes up for your lack of aggression, you're doing yourself a great disservice. What could have been a well negotiated and relatively painless divorce has now become World War III. You will end up with a large legal bill to be paid monthly as you proceed or taken out from your property distribution. You will end up with bad feelings about your spouse, the legal system, your attorney, and yourself for hiring that jackass in the first place. You are not going to be a happy camper and you are going to suffer a loss of self-esteem by having your divorce turned into this war.

This is not to suggest that you hire the first mild, meek and sweet talking attorney you come across. By no means do I encourage that! You want someone throughly competent and conversant with the legal issues. You want someone who can make a courtroom appearance without fainting, stuttering, or worst of all, ticking off the judge. You want someone who will help **you** make the decisions **you** need to make in order for **you** to reach a satisfactory conclusion to **your** case.

Here's the problem with wanting to hire someone who will make all your decisions for you and perhaps emasculate your husband or turn your wife to gelatin. You have now allowed someone else to take over your life at a time when you desperately need to be in charge of your own affairs. How you handle your divorce will speak volumes as to how you can handle life in general. To abdicate that position by allowing someone else to take charge of your life takes away your dignity and self esteem, reducing you to an incompetent.

In case the incompetent argument is insufficient for you, let me point out a few things about the law you should be aware of before making this crucial legal representation decision. First, since most states have no-fault divorce, the need to hire an aggressive attorney to go for the jugular is unnecessary. The divorce itself is largely a matter of paperwork. The property settlement is a matter of finding and defining assets and then deciding upon the appropriate division based upon criteria set forth in statutes or caselaw in your jurisdiction. Alimony is also a matter of looking at the respective financial status of each party after property distribution and then deciding on an appropriate amount and term.

The messiest and fuzziest of all areas is custody. Most states have a meaningless "best interests of the child" standard. As I wrote earlier, interpretations of that phrase can differ widely. I know that I can parent better than you and you think the same of me. Given this standard that you can drive a legal truck through, this is an area where level headedness is most needed. Sometimes a strong dose of reality checking is required.

Divorce with Dignity
Kathleen Berge Entenmann

The shark will gladly tell an absentee father to go for full custody (whatever that is) and attempt to take punitive actions against the mother. An attorney with a solid family law back round in custody law will advise the absentee father that his notions about gaining full custody (whatever that is) are wrongheaded and that he should abandon any notion that he is going to gain custody away from the full-time custodial mother, regardless of how upset he is that she now wants a divorce, support and property distribution.

Right or wrong, fault has little to do with how our courts are going to decide these issues unless the fault involved is so egregious and the conduct so inhumane that a judge is compelled to punish the other spouse. Quite simply, your hurt feelings about your partner's misconduct will not matter legally. Judges do not enjoy listening to a litany of complaints from litigants and they generally look for the easiest and sanest way of resolving conflict. In many instances, your tale of woe will be ruled irrelevant and not even be brought forth in testimony. So why would you hire an attorney who's going to pump up your bile only to have these issues go unaddressed in court?

Even if your case is one not headed for court, (by the way, only a small percentage do) you still don't want to hire someone intent on making marital misconduct the centerpiece of the negotiations. As I earlier stated, guilt works for only a short period. When it wears off, the guilty party begins to rationalize their bad behavior until everything that went wrong becomes your fault. Don't open this door. Bringing guilt or the threat of exposure of marital misconduct will not go far and will only inflame passions that drive your divorce from one that can be easily settled to one that will drag you both through the legal system. At the end, you both will have significant debt for legal fees. Do you want to waste your money this way?

Divorce with Dignity
Kathleen Berge Entenmann

I stated earlier that a shark does not consider the emotional costs involved in a divorce. If you think about it, almost every human transaction carries more than one cost. These can be characterized as financial, emotional, physical, temporal or spiritual. If I want to buy a new outfit, I have to go to the store, try on clothes, risk emotional harm when I seek nothing fits or looks right, take time away from busy schedule, and pay money I may not be able to really afford. What seemed like a good idea when I read the ads for the clearance sales may become a waste of time and a disappointment.

So too with all the transactions involved with your divorce. Is it worth spending your time arguing over who gets the living room furniture and who gets the family room furniture? Is it worth the emotional hassle involved in arguing that your children return home every night by 8:30 pm sharp? Is it worth the knot in your stomach to fight your wife over an additional $50.00 per month support? And is it worth the mounting legal fees?

The answers to some of these questions may be a legitimate yes, in which case, go for it. But if the answer is no, don't allow your attorney to pull you into a position that doesn't make sense when you consider all the transactional costs. You may be getting into something that will cost you far more than you bargained for. That cost may also include trips to a therapist to contend with the emotional backlash from dealing with issues that could have been resolved more easily, Will your attorney be visiting your therapist with you? Think about it.

Earlier I stated that you need an attorney who will assist you in making the decisions you need to make in this divorce. This implies finding someone who relates to you, who speaks in plain English, who explains the substantive law (your rights and responsibilities) as well as the process (how to get from point A to point B in the legal world).

Divorce with Dignity
Kathleen Berge Entenmann

You have an absolute right to ask questions and expect intelligible answers not hidden in a fog of legal gobbledygook. Whether from a need to appear superior or from sheer incompetence, the shark will hide responses in legal jargon, half-truths or outright deceptions. If you don't understand what you've been told, ask again. Demand plain English. And if you still don't understand, don't get out the dictionary, get out the phone book. Get thee to new counsel!

And if you're impressed by the language used by your attorney, don't be. Everyone with a law degree knows this language. No one is going to be wowed by lawyer speak, not the other lawyer, the judge or a hearing officer. Demand clear language and answers! (But don't expect guarantees. There are no such things as I'm constantly reminded when a judge or hearing officer with a different mindset decides against a client who I think has a sure winner.)

Divorce with Dignity
Kathleen Berge Entenmann

In the previous chapter I wrote about friends and family who prompt and encourage you to engage in spouse bashing. Some attorneys also get a kick watching your blood boil when you engage in cathartic verbal bloodletting. Don't let yours do this!

With that warning, you still need to voice your opinions and feelings about your spouse with your attorney. Often the real truths central to your case are hidden in these outpourings. A good attorney will keep you focused on the important issues when you get carried away, screaming about your no-good, control freak spouse. Is your real concern about your ex-spouse's constant disregard of custody times a concern over bedtimes on school nights or are you more concerned that your spouse is pushing your buttons? Are you upset that your ex-spouse is a cheapskate because he/she never buys the children clothing, or do you have a legitimate need for additional financial assistance? Are you worried that your ex-spouse is a spendthrift and that alimony checks will be spent on frivolities and the mortgage will go unpaid, or do you just resent writing the check every month?

More often than not, I find legitimate complaints hidden in the rambling and emotional tales of my clients. You need an attorney who will listen to your outpourings of fear, anger, depression, grief and shock in order to ascertain what's really wrong (or right) with your life and help you make decisions that you need to make and are comfortable with.

In cases involving children, you need an attorney who helps you focus on the fact that you will continue to have a relationship with your spouse. You need someone who acknowledges and respects the fact that even though you are divorcing and dealing with difficult matters, matters sometimes made even more difficult by your spouse, you need to maintain at least a civil relationship with that person. For the next several years, even beyond the majority of your children, you two will be dealing

with each other on a number of kid issues from school,
to weddings, to career advice. The fighting that
continues between divorced parents is what drives their
adult children to take ski or tropical vacations when the
holidays arrive. They don't want to be in the cross-fire
or listen to the constant complaining.

Remembering that you will have a long term
relationship with your ex-spouse is difficult to accept
when you feel taken advantage of by your spouse. In
these times you don't need someone who is fanning the
flames of your righteous indignation with hollow
promises of legal redress, when in fact, the conduct does
not amount to contempt of court or a breach of an
agreement. Sometimes stuff falls into the "shit happens"
category when you're dealing with an asshole. You do
need someone who can sort the legitimate got-to-file-for-
sanctions-and-go-to-court actions from those a judge
cannot address.

Divorce with Dignity
Kathleen Berge Entenmann

Sometimes the only advice an attorney can give you is "I have no piece of paper and I know of no judge who has a piece of paper that can stop your spouse from being an ass if he/she chooses." As much as we would like to believe that there is a legal remedy for every wrong, this simply is not the truth. A person can be skirting the bounds of a legal agreement or court order, but still be within the bounds. Pursuing a contempt petition or modification action could prove an expensive and fruitless adventure. Better that you accept that this person will always be there acting like a jerk and the best you can do is carry on (or as Churchill would say, "KBO - Keep Buggering On). Show that their actions do not affect you. Take away their little game by not playing along. And have an attorney who recognizes this truth as well and helps you get through this with as little pain as possible.

Recap time: Keep the following in mind when hiring an attorney

- Hire someone who will not engage you in a protracted battle over fault since in most states this is irrelevant.

- Hire someone who understands the transactional costs involved that go beyond financial gain or loss, but include an emotional price as well.

- Hire an attorney who understands you and whom you can understand as well.

- Hire an attorney who is not out to fuel the emotional fire but is willing to listen to your opinions and feeling concerning your spouse.

How do you know the attorney you're considering meets these criteria? Ask questions during the first interview. First ask about fault and whether you have to prepare a case centered on this issue. Does the attorney appear interested in the sordid details for reasons other than ferreting out whether you may have other legal actions? Does the attorney seem interested and empathetic when listening to you?

Next ask about the attorney's philosophy concerning client care. Is the attorney interested in winning at all costs? Is there any acknowledgement of the emotional costs of this proceeding? Listen to the responses. Are they in plain English? Are they condescending or acknowledge that you have some intelligence?

Now let me have my little cathartic moment concerning clients. This is to advise you on how to be, if not the ideal client, a better client so that your attorney can more effectively represent you and not be continually aggrieved by you.

Item One: Even if you have a law degree, don't tell you lawyer what he or she should do in representing you. If you do have a law degree, make sure that you're not representing yourself and defer to your attorney.

This does not mean that you abdicate total control over your case or put all the decision making on your attorney. This **does** mean, however, that when your attorney has advised you of the appropriate way to proceed, you listen and follow the advice. You should expect to have discussions that cover all the hypothetical and potential results in your case. If you raise what happened to your barroom buddy or your cousin Althea in their divorces, don't be shocked when your attorney dismisses your comments. Your attorney didn't represent your buddy or cousin and doesn't know their circumstances. Besides, your buddy and cousin may not have correctly represented what happened in their cases. Exaggerations and misunderstandings have been known to happen.

Ask an exhaustive list of questions. Listen to the advice. Follow the advice. If you're not prepared to do these things, hire another lawyer. Seriously. I realize this is your life and you have the right to make the ultimate decisions about it. That's what I've been encouraging you to do and it's the major thesis of this book. But if you're going to trust a professional to represent you in this matter, and you're satisfied you've chosen the right one then **listen** to their advice. This shouldn't be their first rodeo, even if it's yours, and they should know what they're doing.

Item Two: Don't quote to your attorney the brilliant insights of your mother, father, sister, brother, best friend or barroom buddy, unless your mother, father, sister, brother, best friend or barroom buddy has a law degree. Even then don't quote the insights of your lawyer mother, father, sister, brother, best friend or barroom buddy, unless your mother, father, sister, brother, best friend, or barroom buddy practices in the family division. I can't tell you how many clients have contradicted a point of law I've just cited to them with the following: "But my mother , father, (fill-in-the-blank, et al) told me I wouldn't have to give him any custody if he's not paying child support." It is then that I demand to know where this person is licensed so they can be sued for malpractice or disbarred. Normally, the relative turns out to be a non-lawyer who doesn't know what they're talking about.

I don't know many corporate, criminal or personal lawyers who understand the ins and outs of the family division the way family lawyers who are in the trenches there everyday do. As a family lawyer, I would not be so presumptuous as to represent someone before the SEC or a technical secured transaction case, simply because I own stock. Why choose an attorney to represent you in a divorce simply because they're divorced themselves or they happen to be your friend or relative? Even free representation from a relative ends up exacting a price.

A colleague recently told me about a case in which the other party is represented by a relative. This attorney who has undertaken representation of a sibling in a difficult and contentious custody case has no family law experience. In fact, this attorney who has no family law experience practices bankruptcy law and sneers at the family court practice as being beneath his considerable legal talents. Armed with arrogance and ignorance, this attorney has now dragged out this case and filed frivolous motions that have only served to further poison an already toxic situation. And a desire to show off for a sibling has turned the case into a litigious morass.

The other problem with representation by a family member is the client's tendency not to follow the advice. Some time ago, a friend told me, and it's absolutely true, that family members come asking for legal advice (free of course) from you, the nephew, niece, brother, sister, or cousin attorney. Weeks or months later you ask them what's happened with their legal problem and if the advice worked. "Well, Cousin Fred, (the machinist who's only legal experience is from watching "Law and Order") told me to do the exact opposite, so that's what I did. " No joke. Now your relative has a situation that's ten times worse and has to be represented by an expensive law firm simply because they didn't want to follow your advice from the start.

In this case, the only solace you can take from the situation is that at least the advice was free. But what if you paid for that advice and decided to ignore it in favor of Cousin Fred's suggestions? Now you have additional attorney fees that might have been avoided through following through on your attorney's initial recommendations. Maybe your attorney has dropped you because you don't want to follow their advice and you undermine what your attorney is attempting to negotiate. Now you have to start over again with new counsel. Sound like fun?

Item Three: Don't expect your attorney to get sucked up into your emotional tornado. Attorneys can't function as professionals if they react emotionally to your problems. Again, this does not mean you shouldn't reveal your opinions and feelings about what's happening or relate unpleasant exchanges you and your spouse have. This is often where the truth is revealed that can help your attorney resolve your problems. But by the same token, don't expect your attorney to be the playground bully who exchanges harsh words, rude behavior, and dirty looks with your spouse and counsel. That won't help your case. And it's not fair to expect your attorney to beat up on your spouse and opposing counsel. It's unprofessional and unnecessary.

It's also unfair of you to ask your attorney to take home your problems with them. We all have enough personal baggage we put aside during the day to focus on our clients. At the end of the day we have to deal with that personal baggage, not yours.

Item Four: Pay your attorney. One of the quickest ways to find yourself on the back burner in an attorney's office is to ignore the polite, insistent, demanding, threatening requests for payment. When your attorney realizes that you have no intention to pay the very next step is withdrawing from the

representation.

Some of the excuses for non-payment

demonstrate how either a client has not read the fee

agreement letter signed by the client or paid attention to

the advice given. "All I wanted was a simple no-fault

divorce." Yes, and you weren't able to assist in locating

your spouse so that the necessary papers could be served,

it turned out you had considerable assets that you two

really hadn't agreed to divide, or your thoughts about

custody were significantly different.

Your attorney's bill should not be a shock to you

if you carefully listened to your attorney and read the

retainer letter that sets forth the rates and fees to be

charged. Make sure you have a retainer letter; every

attorney should provide one covering both the financial

arrangements between client and attorney as well as

what matter will be covered in the representation.

During the course of your case if other issues arise that

agreement can be amended or a new one drafted to cover an unrelated matter such as a personal injury or criminal action.

Most retainer letters state that your attorney will bill for all services performed, including phone calls and letters in addition to the pleadings and court representation. So don't be surprised when your bill lists all the phone calls you made to your attorney. Don't think that every piece of correspondence comes without a price tag; it does. Don't think your witty banter in the court house hallway will reduce the fees for attending a hearing; it won't. Respect the fact that this is your attorney's livelihood and if it weren't for the time being spent on your case, it could be spent on someone else's behalf who does respect invoices and makes timely payments.

Another reason clients give for non-payment is the attitude once a matter has been successfully resolved that they could have done this on their own. Right.

Divorce with Dignity
Kathleen Berge Entenmann

Your relationship with your spouse has become so
dysfunctional that you can't agree on anything, and you
could have resolved this on your own. This is
reminiscent of people who have no clue what to do in a
given situation, ask for an opinion, and then declare
that's what they were thinking all along. Clueless, yet
brilliant. Right.

Also, don't expect a Ferrari for Fiesta prices. If
you have a complicated
case that includes pleadings, motions and litigation,
expect to pay for these services. If you feel you've been
gouged, discuss the bill with your attorney and if you are
still unsatisfied the local bar association has a fee dispute
committee to air your complaint. But please don't
expect your attorney to engage in litigation, prepare
pleadings, hold numerous meeting, answer phone calls
and only charge you for a fraction of the time spent.
That is totally unrealistic.

Divorce with Dignity
Kathleen Berge Entenmann

By the way, now is not the time to be cheap

when it comes to hiring a lawyer. Many is the client

who's come to my office after seeing a "no frills" attorney

who charged a minimal fee for filing a no-fault divorce.

Their legal services did not include a comprehensive

property settlement agreement, temporary spousal

support or alimony representation. Oftentimes these

complaints were filed in counties several miles away

where litigating these claims would be not only infeasible

but legally objectionable. Many people think that they

only thing they need is the divorce decree and ignore

these other issues. Their failure to get counsel that will

complete the necessary work leaves then in the position

of now trying to negotiate issues where there may be no

legal recourse since the matter had to be raised in the

initial pleadings. These clients were either not advised of

or ignored the written warnings on the pleadings of the

need to raise these matters before a final divorce decree

was entered. Now they are left with a much more

difficult situation than if the divorce had proceeded initially with all the issues raised. Bottom line - get someone to do it right the first time. It will cost you more initially than the cheapie divorce, but in the long run you will save money in those transactional costs.

If you keep these items in minds, you and your non-shark attorney will have a professional and cordial relationship. You may not walk off an airplane tarmac into the night fog, arm in arm like Bogart and Raines, but you'll resolve your problems effectively.

Tasks for Step Six

1.	Prior to your initial consultation, make an exhaustive list of all questions you want to ask the attorney. Include specific questions about your circumstances (custody, support, property).

2.	When you speak with your attorney, make sure you have a thorough understanding of the legal fees involved and the scope of representation.

3.   Once you have a feel from your attorney about the expected fees involved, make sure you have sufficient funds to pay. If you do not, be honest and ask the attorney if a payment plan can be worked out.

4.   Be prepared at some point, preferably before your initial consultation to prepare a history of your marriage including employment histories for both of you, important dates (birth of children, date of marriage, respective birth dates of spouses), nature and location of assets. Make sure you've gathered as much critical information as you can, especially social security numbers.

5.   Organize your thoughts prior to consulting with your attorney, be it for the first time or during the representation. Don't call in a panicked state! Take the time to think through the

situation and then call with a coherent request

or agenda.

Samantha took Ben's old legal pad and began to

write the questions she would ask the next day.

Lawyer Questions

1. *What is your experience in this area?*

2. *I think we've resolved custody but Ben*

   occasionally makes noises about changing it.

   How often is he allowed to do this?

3. *I heard that I might be able to get a part*

   of his pension/ 40k. Really?

4. *I can't afford this house, but I want to*

   stay here. Can this happen?

5. *Cynthia and Edward are both headed for*

   college. Does this need to be in an

   agreement?

6. What about my health insurance?

7. Will I have to go to work? Can I go back

to school? I think I need some more

skills.

8. Can I stop Ben from having the kids

exposed to his various girlfriends?

Samantha's made two appointments for the day,
hoping she could decide between two lawyers and could
get this odious task out of the way in a swift and efficient
manner. Her first appointment was with a lawyer
referred by her friend Nick, her financial planner. Nick
had worked with this attorney, Michael Velli, on other
divorce cases in the past. Nick raved about Velli's take
no prisoner attitude and his ability to get the most money
for his client. Nick wasn't sure if Velli did any custody
work since their working relationship concerned property
cases.

Samantha drove straight downtown after
dropping off the kids, arriving thirty minutes early for her
appointment with Attorney Velli. Velli's secretary, Lisa,

gave Samantha directions to their office building from the garage she recommended. It took Samantha most of those thirty minutes to walk the long blocks from the garage. She was thankful for the flats on her feet. High heels might have killed her.

As she got off the elevator and headed for the office door of Velli, Machi and Prince, she heard loud yelling coming from inside their offices. More than a few obscenities were sprinkled throughout the torrent of verbal abuse that anyone on that floor could plainly hear. Timidly, Samantha entered the office and was greeted by the young receptionist, Becky.

"Hi, I'm Samantha. I have a 9:30 appointment with Mr. Velli." The yelling was even louder inside the office area than out in the hall. Who was the maniac making all that noise?

"Have a seat. He'll be done soon. Let me take your coat. Would you like some coffee or tea or a glass of water?"

"Water, please," Samantha responded. She didn't want her mouth to go completely dry during the interview.

Becky returned with the water and reassured Samantha that Mr. Velli was almost done with his phone call. "Shit," Samantha thought, "he must be the maniac yelling and screaming."

A few minutes later a short well dressed man with a bright red complexion came out of the offices and into the reception area. "Hi," he greeted Samantha, "I'm Mike Velli. Won't you come back." His voice was a quieter version of the one screaming on the phone.

Samantha sat in the wing back client chair that faced the huge leather office chair across the beautiful mahogany desk in Velli's office. She placed her water glass on the coaster he slid across the desk. Thus began her painful ordeal.

"So you're Nick's friend," Velli began. "Great financial planner. A real genius. I keep my personal portfolio with him."

"Yeah, Nick's great. My husband Ben and I have invested with him for years."

"My secretary tells me you're here for a divorce consultation. What's happening?"

Samantha recited her carefully prepared speech about the events that led her to his moment. She emphasized her financial needs, both support and property. She mentioned Ben's infidelity but didn't dwell on it. She had the feeling that Mr. Velli was not the soul of discretion, especially when he had already discussed her life with Nick. She dabbed away a few tears; talking about her kids always made her misty, especially when she felt protective of them.

"Yeah, Nick told me about your husband. I'm going to make him pay for what he did." Mike Velli began his blustering. "He won't know what hit him. I foresee you ending up with 80% of the assets, lifetime alimony, and him paying full freight for your kids."

"Really?" Samantha asked dumbfounded. "My attorney for the support case seemed to think that an equitable division of assets might get me 60% or so, but not 80%. He also felt that I was not entitled to lifetime alimony and that I may have to shoulder some of the burden with the kids."

"Nonsense. I know your prior attorney - always trying to settle cases on the cheap. Anyone with some guts is going to fight this out and get you every last dime your husband's been spending on his women."

"That sounds an awful lot like revenge. I'm not interested in revenge. I want both of us to be able to get along after this and I don't see that happening if we go to war."

"What makes you think this will be war? He's a respected member of the bar. The last thing he wants is for this to get around town."

"Get around town? I thought these matters were handled in confidence."

"Yeah right," Velli sneered. "Closed door hearings and by the late afternoon, everyone in town knows everyone's business. Tipstaffs talk, secretaries talk, lawyers talk, hell, even judges talk. You put a lawyer through Family Division and everyone's going to know about it."

"Shit," Samantha said out loud. "Sorry 'bout that. This can't become public."

"That's why we're going to hit him hard. Load up a pleading with every count we can think of. Threaten hearings if he doesn't come around to our way of thinking. Make him sweat."

"*Jesus*," Samantha thought, "I don't need this. I've got to deal with Ben the rest of my life, or at least for the next several years."

"Mr. Velli, maybe you could explain to me the law and how you see this happening," Samantha gave the blowhard the chance to explain his strategy in the case. For the next thirty minutes straight Velli outlined the law, emphasizing his theories about wronged wives receiving all the assets. He did mention that he seldom saw that happen, but with the right judge, who knew?

"Thank you, Mr. Velli, for your time. I'll let you know what I decide to do." Samantha stood and shook hands with the lawyer.

"Before you go, don't you want to know about my fees?" Velli had an almost pleading tone to his voice.

"I think we both know that won't be necessary." With that, Samantha strode out the door, grabbing her coat from Becky and heaving s heavy sigh. "If I were Goldilocks, he would be too hard," she smiled to herself.

Once out the door, she headed to the building's coffee shop and ordered a vanilla latte and cinnamon scone. Her head hurt from the appointment; Mike Valli was arrogant, somewhat rude, and definitely loud. She wondered if these traits were the result of a complex over his size.

As she was nibbling and sipping, she spotted Ben walking through the lobby. She jumped off her stool and ran to the entrance. He turned and saw her as she called his name.

"What are you doing here?" Ben asked. Samantha's whereabouts were seldom disclosed to him and he seemed visibly surprised to see her.

"Had an appointment with Mike Velli... Nick referred him to me."

Ben groaned. "That asshole? What promises did he make you?"

"Well, I don't want to disclose the confidential conversation I just had, but apparently I can clean you out." Samantha held her deadpan expression for three seconds and then began to laugh. "Don't worry. I found the man odious to say the least. Not for me."

Ben looked as though he was about to kiss her. "Thank God. We don't need Mike Velli in our lives."

"I know. I've been reading this book *Divorce with Dignity*, and while I don't agree with everything, I agree with the chapter about lawyers. He seems to fall into the shark category and would just just run up my bill."

"You're reading that too? My secretary gave me her copy from her divorce. She said it helped her and her ex get along better after the divorce than before. I've just started it. And I agree with you about Velli and legal fees; that's his reputation."

"Ben, I know I need a lawyer. But honestly, as much as you've hurt me and made me soooo mad, I don't want to fight you in court. Is there someway we can work this out?"

"Sam you're right about the lawyer. But there's no reason why we can't work out an amicable settlement. But you need representation. As your former lawyer, I advise you to get one." Ben smiled, relieved that Samantha didn't want war and held out the prospect for a peaceful resolution.

"I have another appointment today, after lunch. I thought I'd do some shopping and then see the next attorney."

"Do you mind telling me who?"

"It's Morgan Plowman. My friend Michelle used her for her divorce. Ever hear of her?"

"Yeah. Her name was suggested to me before I decided to go in-house with Dave Simmons. She has a good reputation in the bar. Apparently she knows what she's doing, is easy to work with and gets good results. Her clients seem to love her."

"Well, I'm seeing her at two. For a change, the kids are getting home on their own."

"How are they?" Ben reluctantly asked, expecting a bitch out for the last visit he had with the kids.

"Okay," Samantha responded. She wanted to add *"no thanks to you,"* but left that thought unspoken. "They had a major melt down after they last saw you. But they recovered and it appears there's no permanent damage."

"What did you say to them?" Ben asked.

"I should ask you the same, but I think I've got the gist of it. I told them we were not reconciling, you wanted a new life, but we would always be there for them. They also needed to know that they were not the cause of this divorce and that we both love them." Samantha started to tear up but managed to keep it together. She started to get off her stool to leave.

"Thanks, Sam. I appreciate you being there for them. You've always been a great mother."

"Well, I've always known that you thought of me as a *mother*. Sometimes the feeling is mutual," Samantha joked.

"Ouch. I deserve that. But I'm glad you're going to see Morgan. Dave and I would like to resolve this peacefully, if we can."

"Me too. Believe it or not, after what you put this family through, I'm not out for blood. Otherwise I would have retained Velli.

"Would you like me to pick up the kids from school and take them out to dinner? Maybe we can even catch an early movie."

"Sure. Text them so they know you're coming. And try to find out if they have homework tonight. They may have to do that instead of a movie."

"Great. Catch you later." With that Ben was out the door, on his way to wherever. Samantha didn't need to know or care to know. He was becoming an amicable stranger whom she happened to be married to at one time. His business was his, hers was hers. Maybe they could work this out.

Divorce with Dignity
Kathleen Berge Entenmann

Samantha spent the next few hours browsing through the large downtown Macy's. She looked at everything from shoes and outfits for herself, to housewares and gadgets for home. She thought about looking at clothes for Cynthia and Edward, but knew they wouldn't appreciate her purchases. Even if she copied the questionable clothing they usually chose for themselves, that teenage rebellion would immediately reject a Mom purchase. Just as well..she worried a little about money, even though Ben was faithful with the support.

After lunch in one of the store's restaurants, Samantha headed over to the offices of Plowman and Richter. Even though she was fifteen minutes early, she decided she would wait in their reception area. She had tired of walking and shopping. Maybe they had some decent magazines.

When Samantha walked in she was immediately greeted by the firm's receptionist, Laurie. "Could I take your coat?" she offered and hung it in the closet. "Would you like some coffee, tea, soft drink or water?"

"A cup of tea would be great. It's a little cold out there."

Divorce with Dignity
Kathleen Berge Entenmann

"Earl Grey, Constant Comment, Lemon Lift or plain old Lipton's?"

"Oh, I love Constant Comment. Thanks."

Samantha settled into the corner of the sofa next to the end table. She looked over the reading selections, all current editions of popular magazines from Time to Sports Illustrated to People. She also spotted a well-worn edition of *Divorce with Dignity*, but decided to choose a recent Esquire instead. She missed reading the copies Ben would bring home.

Laurie once more appeared. "Here's your tea. We have some cookies in case you're interested. Mr. Richter is a bit of an anglophile and likes to have an afternoon tea with the staff. Would you like some?"

"No thanks. I had dessert with lunch which I almost never do. I'm probably on a sugar rush right now." Samantha didn't know why she felt the need to offer this information as she thought about the classic chicken ala king and the sky high ice cream pie she just ate. Coming downtown was dangerous to her waistline.

"Ms. Plowman knows you're here. She'll be out in a moment."

"Thanks." With that, Samantha turned to an article about the New Orleans Jazz Festival and the reviews of the various performers. She'd have to look for the festival cd that was coming out. Maybe an early Christmas present for herself, or a suggestion for the kids' gift to Ben. They never knew what he wanted, especially since he always told them not to bother.

Samantha had just lifted her cup for a sip when Morgan Plowman appeared. She wore a smart pantsuit tastefully accessorized by a few pieces of jewelry. A large ring hung on a chain around her neck. Morgan noticed Samantha staring at it. "That's a gift from my kids. It's a replica of the ring from Lord of the Rings. It even has the beautiful inscription." Morgan held the ring up for Samantha's closer inscription.

"Beautiful," Samantha offered. "I love those books and the movies."

"Me too. We're planning a trip to New Zealand to see where it was filmed. Can't wait. Laurie, could you take Samantha's tea back to my office and bring the pot?" With that Morgan turned around, ushering Samantha to her office for their consultation. Samantha wondered how tough this session would be. It would have to be better than the Velli consultation.

"So, Samantha, do you want to give me an idea of what's going on?"

"How much detail do you need?" Samantha wasn't sure she could go through another emotional outburst.

"As much as you want to. Please know that everything you tell me is in confidence. I take that very seriously. Would you feel more comfortable if I just asked you questions?" Morgan was giving Samantha an opportunity to make this as pain free as she could.

"How about if I ask you the questions I have?"

"Okay. I'll answer yours and then you answer mine."

So Samantha proceeded to launch into the pressing questions on her mind. Custody - reviewable with a change of circumstances. Child support - modifiable with a change of circumstances. . Property settlement - expect around 60-70%. House - maybe she and the kids could stay there until they were through college, the sell it and split the proceeds. Alimony - non-modifiable unless the parties agree or the court orders.

Amount and duration vary depending on the property

distribution and the individual circumstances. Attorney

fees - Ben might have to pay all or the court could look

at the property distribution. The client is still primarily

responsible. Future girlfriends - in the picture unless they

endanger the kids.

Morgan agreed that Nick would be a valuable

resource for working out the financial planning. After all,

he knew better than anyone else the extent of their

assets. Maybe he could do a quick work-up for Ben and

Samantha that Ben could pay for without a trip to court.

Morgan then asked Samantha some basic

questions to fill in various dates and events. Samantha

was prepared with the answers and breezed through

that part of the interview. Morgan then gently pried out

information concerning Ben's infidelity and the current

custody status. She made few comments, simply

nodding her head and taking notes.

Samantha then asked Morgan the question that

sealed the deal. "I saw *Divorce with Dignity* in your

waiting room. Do you recommend it to your clients?"

"That's why it's there. Have you read it?"

"Most of it. I try to take it one step at a time and do the exercises at the end of the steps. I just finished the lawyer step."

"You did well. You were well prepared with your questions. You may want to read the next step, though - **Mediate, don't Litigate.** I'm a major proponent of mediation, if the parties are open to it."

"What is it?" Samantha had heard the term but was unfamiliar with the process.

"Read the chapter and then we'll talk. I know a mediator who's worked on some of my prior cases. There's nothing urgent happening right now and you and Ben may want to try this before pleadings are filed and litigation started. Think about it."

"What about your retainer?"

"I'll send you a letter. As we discussed, my hourly rate is $250 and I'll need an initial retainer of $2500 for the first ten hours. I'll spell out everything in the letter."

"Fine. I'll probably call after I've received your letter and read about mediation. I really don't want to get into a lot of litigation."

"Look forward to hearing from you."

"Thanks for your time. This wasn't nearly as bad as I thought it would be."

"Thanks, I guess. Talk to you later."

Samantha left feeling better than she had for some time. She had some work to do and an important conversation to have with Ben. Maybe this wouldn't be that bad.

Chapter Ten

Samantha awoke in the near dark. Her feet were ready to move her into her morning maneuvers. Her head wanted to stay on the pillow for a few more winks and some time to sober up. Thank God today was not a school day and there was no urgent need to leave bed.

Yesterday, when she got home from her downtown appointments, she was greeted with a note from Cynthia.

Hey mom, the geek and I are going out with Dad for dinner and a movie. We should be home by ten. Homework's done. Dad wants to talk to you when we get back.

Love, C

Samantha then went to the freezer for a Lean Cuisine, popped it in the microwave, poured a glass of scotch, and seated herself at the dining room table. She had heard a news story about how people who are suddenly alone should treat themselves to a meal, served as though there were others around, and not stand over the kitchen sink or counters eating. Samantha then decided to make eating alone the same ritual as eating with the kids. She usually set a place for herself at the table, used the everyday stoneware instead of paper plates, and served herself a glass of wine. Tonight she needed a Dewars. What a day.

In a few minutes her dinner was nuked, served and eaten. She put the dishes into thedishwasher, grabbed her Dewars, and headed into the living room. She knew she'd have to read the mediation chapter before Ben returned with the kids so they could discuss the possibilities. She also needed money from Ben for Morgan's retainer as she anticipated the letter arriving in the next few days. Will the fun never end today?

Samantha sat down with the book, looking forward to this step. She was happy her attorney approved of mediation. What would Ben think? Would the big attorney want to work things out with her? Was she up to sitting down with Ben?

STEP SEVEN - MEDIATE, DON'T LITIGATE

Your willingness to sit down with your spouse

and work out a mediated settlement may

eliminate the need for any litigation and

demonstrates your sense of strength, confidence

and self respect

Mediation is an idea whose time has definitely

come, and yet many people ignore this method for

dispute resolution that can keep them out of the

courtroom and reduce the need for attorney services. I

said reduce the need, not eliminate the need, because the

two of you will need attorneys for advice as well as the

preparation of any necessary agreements or legal

documents. But you will reduce your overall attorney

expense because instead of the two of you paying for

two attorneys who talk to each other and not you two,

you can hire a mediator who will meet with both of you

and assist in reaching a resolutions of your issues.

Divorce with Dignity
Kathleen Berge Entenmann

You will also stop playing the child's game of Telephone where one person starts a message which gets passed along through others until it reaches the last person in a chain of communication. The fun part of the game is to hear how garbled the message and distorted the message becomes when announced at the end. Not so fun when your life is involved.

So instead of playing games, you and your spouse meet face to face, speaking directly to each other with the assistance of a third party, a mediator. The mediator's job is to help transmit or refine the message so that it comes out crystal clear. Both of you should be heard and understood and the mediator is there to make sure that happens.

What mediation is not: Many people confuse mediation with arbitration which is another dispute resolution device. In arbitration the parties agree to allow a "neutral" person or panel hear their dispute. Some arbitrations strictly adhere to courtroom procedures, following the rules and laws of evidence and case presentation. Others are somewhat less formal, oftentimes with both sides submitting their evidence by stipulations and allowing the trier of fact to decide the outcome. No matter what the format, however, you are in a litigious situation which in some ways may be better than going to court before a judge. But arbitration still gives the decision making power to an outsider, not you.

What is mediation? Simply put, it is one of several means to resolve or handle conflict where the parties engage the services of a third person to facilitate discussion and reach an understanding. A mediator does not the authority to resolve your conflict as would a judge or arbitrator. A mediator does not act as an attorney; legal or professional services are not provided beyond facilitating discussion between you and your spouse. A mediator should not draft a legal agreement, consent order of court, or any other legally enforceable document. A mediator should not represent either or both of you in any legal proceeding. A mediator should simply be the third party in the room while you and your spouse get through the business of discussing the issues you need to resolve.

Will the mediator be neutral? In all likelihood, no. The mediator is like any other human being with prejudices and interests that extend beyond your situation and your issues. Accordingly, the mediator will bring those prejudices and interests into the room and probably express them. As a mother of two, I could not sit by quietly during a mediation if one parent suggested that child care for children under twelve is unnecessary. I would probably have a thing or two to say to the parent who does not want to budget for after school child care and wants to allow the children to become latch key kids. I would hope to make my objection in such a fashion that the person who made the suggestion does not feel idiotic or enraged and the other parent virtuous and vindicated. Both sides have to feel they are making a collaborative effort.

The mediator's function is to allow both sides to speak so that their issues are heard and to manage the process of resolving those issues in an efficient and productive manner. The mediator should be aware of power imbalances that make one or the other timid and unable to freely express themselves. Both sides need to be comfortable with the process and not feel as though they are being railroaded into an agreement. The mediator should make clear when thr are two sides to an issue and help both sides articulate their position without advocating for one over the other. The mediator must see that both sides are given a fair hearing without ridicule or scorn.

Take the previous after school child care example. Let's assume this issue came up in the context of spousal/child support. Mother has always been a stay-at-home mom for her two children who are now eight and ten. The eight year old is a real pistol who is very self-confident and isn't afraid to let the world know that she isn't afraid of anyone or anything. The ten year old is far more introspective and cautious about everyone and everything. Dad thinks it's time for Mom to leave the nest, finish her college degree and find a job. Mom thinks that she should still be at home everyday, and besides, Dad doesn't earn enough to afford child care while she's at school. Dad then raises the idea of the children becoming latch key kids who get themselves home from school everyday and stay in the house alone until one of the parents can get there. Mom goes ballistic.

What does the mediator do? Gang up with Mom against Dad? Give some validity to Dad's suggestion? Explore all the possibilities of Mom attending school, perhaps online, and still be able to be with the kids? Given the mediator's background, probably a little of each. Someone has to bring rational debate to this topic. Possible solutions should be

discussed including whether the children are capable of

spending a short time, no more than two hours, alone. Is

there a neighbor or relative who could be there? Are

there affordable after school programs where the

children attend? The mediator should not automatically

shoot down Dad's suggestion or Mom's concern, but be

prepared to get both parties to rationally discuss their

issues for the sake of the children as well as the economic

well-being of the family. Sometimes the mediator feels

like a cafeteria monitor, stopping a food fight. As long as

the parties can become rational again, it's worth getting

hit by some flying mashed potatoes.

This is a very small microcosm as to how a

mediator handles a problem. How the process is

structured will differ from mediator to mediator and

from client to client. Some mediators like to have a tight

control over an agenda and will structure time allotted

for discussion of each item on that agenda. Others will

allow the clients to structure the agenda according to their immediate concerns and needs. Some will suggest solutions and answers while others will prod the clients to exhaust their own brains in reaching solutions and answers.

How do you choose a mediator? As with a therapist or lawyer, first look for recommendations. Talk to your attorney who should be aware of the existence of mediation and may even have a referral list for you. Mediation has gained popularity with courts who would much rather have the litigants resolve their problems outside the courtroom. Many judges have their own referral lists for people they view as likely candidates for this form of conflict resolution. Judges are only too happy to have you keep your problems your own to be resolved through your efforts, not theirs.

Check the background of the person whom you're considering. Is this a lawyer, former judge, mental health professional, clergy or business person? You may want a lawyer with a business background if the issues involve technical legalistic consequences such as division of property or the tax implications of dividing a retirement account. In these matters you may not want a mental health professional who might be incompetent to offer you thorough guidance with these questions. On the other hand, if you're mainly discussing "Life" issues such as parenting arrangements, you may prefer that mental health professional who brings expertise in sociology and psychology when discussing how a particular schedule may affect your child's developing psyche. You and your spouse need to decide which personality and expertise better suits you.

Notwithstanding the previous, don't be surprised if you've misjudged the mediator's ability to deal with your issues based on their background. Simply because a mediator is an attorney does not mean they are comfortable with money issues; their practice may concentrate on custody and they're more in tune with the parenting issues. And more than one mental health professional is savvy about the stock market and business issues while being somewhat dogmatic and unrealistic in their approach to parenting. So have a frank discussion with your potential mediator to find out not only their professional background, but their interests and areas of competence.

Clients also consider the mediator's gender as well as personality when selecting one. Quite often certain assumptions are made that a female mediator will side with the female and the male mediator with the male. I'm often approached by male clients who want a female lawyer or mediator who can neutralize whatever gender bias they perceive. While I don't usually agree with this reasoning, I'm grateful for the new client. Be careful of your personal prejudices and assumptions about these professionals based solely on sex. You may find them incorrect and off-base with the individual you choose.

You should know up front the hourly rate your mediator will charge and whether this represents a savings over the amount you and your spouse would be paying for two attorneys. In most instances, when you and your spouse hire a mediator, you will reach an understanding more quickly and with less expense than if you and your attorney negotiated back and forth with your spouse's attorney. Just as you would with hiring an attorney, be clear as to the fee structure, whether or not a retainer is required, and who is responsible for payment - you, your spouse or both or you.

What will be expected of me in mediation? You should expect to speak your mind frankly on issues under negotiation. There is nothing more frustrating than to have a mediation controlled by one spouse with the other's tacit permission because that spouse refuses to speak up and sits there with a "whatever" attitude. The mediator is then put in the position of forcing words out of the passive participant, making sure there is a mutual understanding and not a railroading by the more aggressive and assertive spouse. The passive spouse can also totally sabotage the mediation by refusing to wholly cooperate and then having his/her attorney nullify any understanding by refusing to commit to an agreement.

You should be willing to commit your time and energy to this process in order to give mediation a fair chance of succeeding. Don't go into this process with the attitude that you're only doing this to appease your spouse if that's who made the suggestion to mediate. It may be better for you to scrap this process altogether than to be dragged into it by someone with whom you're having difficulty. If your reluctance is not dissolved after your first meeting with the mediator, be honest and bag this process. It just might not be for you.

You are also expected to do your homework for mediation. Homework may consist of anything from preparing a household budget, to locating assets and debts, to providing important medical or school

documents concerning your children. You may be

expected to consult with a financial planner, a teacher or

your lawyer to insure your have a thorough

understanding of an issue before you attempt

negotiation.

Finally, you are expected to make full and

complete disclosure concerning any issue that is the

subject of mediation. When discussing financial matters,

put all the information on the table, the good, the bad

and the ugly, that compose a thorough listing of all

assets, liabilities and debts. When discussing the

children, put forth all relevant information concerning

their well being and needs so that you can frame a

parenting agreement with no hidden agendas or

surprises.

***What about mediating with someone who

physically and mentally abuses me?*** If there is

physical or mental abuse, the trained mediator should

ferret out this information from the beginning and then
refuse to mediate your case. In the first session the
mediator should meet individually with each of you to
determine your respective comfort levels in engaging in
this process. At times an individual is intimidated by
their abusive spouse to mediate because the abusive
spouse is frustrated with attorneys who are not giving in
to their demands.

If there are safety issues which may reduce one's
ability to speak freely or negotiate on a level playing field,
mediation should **not** take place. If you are being
abused, you should not be in this process because the
mediator is **not** your representative; your attorney **is.** A
trained mediator should be able to gracefully end the
mediation without further endangering the threatened
spouse.

*What does mediation have to do with
maintaining my self respect?* Many people are
leery of this process because they view it as one more

opportunity to be taken advantage of by their spouse who always gets their way and always seems to be the better negotiator. Here is your chance to demonstrate that you are equally competent in negotiating. Women who for years have run the household while Mr. CEO has run his business may feel intimidated by having to negotiate with the Chairman of the Board.

The mediator's function in this case is to try to level the playing field so that Mrs. Chairman has equal say and power with Mr. Chairman. And often the truth is that while Mr. Chairman knows all about his business, he is completely in the dark about the household the two of them are trying to divide. She may know much more than he about their living expenses and outstanding bills. He's the one on the short end of the power imbalance because he's in the dark.

If this woman leaves her divorce strictly in the hands of counsel, she may never have the opportunity to deal as an equal with her husband, to show she is not incompetent and prove herself worthy of his respect.

She may never have the experience of speaking for

herself and making decisions by herself. She may never

again have this opportunity for self empowerment.

And the greatest part of this is that she can do

this and do it with a safety net. First, the mediator is

there to make sure she doesn't end up as road kill while

hubby speeds along with his agenda. Second, her

attorney can advise her along the way so that she can

have a thorough understanding of what she's doing.

And finally, she will leave mediation with an

understanding only, *not a legal document*, but a

memorandum that can always be fine tuned or totally

scrapped if she later decides she made the wrong

decisions.

The flip side to this scenario is that Mr.

Chairman may now be able to walk away from this

divorce with the knowledge that he has left a much

stronger spouse than he thought he had during the

marriage. His guilt may be somewhat assuaged knowing that his spouse is competent to handle her own affairs. He may also appreciate the fact that the understanding reached was not one he forced through, but one that was intelligently and diligently reached by both of them.

But most importantly, both spouses will avoid the emotional, mental and financial fallout of parading their personal business in front of a judge or having the two attorneys work this out back and forth, back and forth while legal fees for both escalate. If attorneys are necessary to help finalize an understanding or bring clarity to an issue, they can always be invited into the mediation process. But how much better for the couple if they are able to empower themselves to solve their own problems.

Checklist for mediation:

* ***Find out the professional background of the mediator and decide whether or not this suits your particular case.***

- *Make sure you understand the fee structure and who is responsible for payment.*
- *Make sure you are willing to commit your time and energy to this process.*
- *Find out any biases your mediator has that may influence this process.*
- *Make sure you understand the mediation process and how yours will be structured.*
- *Be prepared to disclose all necessary information, whether or not directly requested from you. You may possess information no one has thought of or knows about.*

Tasks for Step Seven

1. Realistically evaluate your ability to negotiate with your spouse. Does the thought of being in the same room for an hour or two with your spouse, even with a third party present, turn your intestinal tract into a

string of knots? If so, you should be honest with the mediator about this issue.

2. If you have already retained an attorney, speak to your counsel about your desire to engage in mediation. If your attorney throws cold water on this process without providing sufficient justification, think seriously about retaining another attorney who will work with you through the mediation.

Samantha considered the information she had just read. Was she a candidate for mediation? Were she and Ben candidates for mediation? Morgan had suggested she read
this step, and now that she had, Samantha thought this may be a good alternative to litigating or even working out matters between counsel.

As she thought about this prospect, Samantha heard the unmistakeable sound of Ben's car in the driveway. The front door opened and there stood Cynthia and Michael with their father framing the doorway.

Divorce with Dignity
Kathleen Berge Entenmann

"Mind if I come in?" Ben asked, somewhat uncertain he was still be received as warmly as he was this morning.

"Sure. Just let me say goodnight to the kids and I'll be right with you." Samantha trailed the kids upstairs, gave each of them a hug and kiss goodnight, and promised to listen to their latest adventures in the morning. They were all looking forward to a trip tomorrow to the science center, a trip Samantha and the kids always enjoyed. Edward in particular was looking forward to the new film at the Omnimax on whales.

Before Samantha left Edward's room, he had to ask. "Mom, are you and Dad getting back together?"

"What makes you think that, sweetie?"

"Well, Dad just seemed to happy over dinner and couldn't wait to talk to you tonight. I thought that was the reason."

"Well, as nice as that might be, your Dad and I have to discuss matters concerning the divorce. We want this to go as smoothly as it can, especially for you and your sister."

"I know, Mom. Just wondering. Good night."

Samantha went downstairs, a little teary as she always was after one of these conversations. What do you say when your child has become the eternal optimist? She hated to burst her son's bubble, but reconciliation was not in the cards. Ben made sure that card was not in the deck, at all.

When she got to the bottom of the stairs, Ben was standing there with two on the rocks glasses. "I saw your empty glass in the living room. I thought I'd refill it and get one for myself. Is that the same Dewars bottle that was here when I left?"

"Yeah. Hardly touched the stuff. I needed one today after meeting with your colleagues in the bar."

"Doesn't sound like a fun day at all. How did things go with Morgan Plowman?" Ben had a hopeful tone to this voice.

"Real good. I think I'm going to retain her. We seem to be on the same wavelength. She also believes that all men are scum." Samantha held her expression for three seconds and then started laughing.

"Okay, I deserve that one too. Seriously, you're really going to retain her?"

Divorce with Dignity
Kathleen Berge Entenmann

"As soon as you give me a check for $2500. I should be receiving her letter by the middle of next week, and that's her requested retainer."

"No problem. It's money well spent if she helps you and me to amicably resolve everything."

"Well, that's another thing I wanted to talk to you about. How do you feel about seeing a mediator to do that?"

"Do you really think we need one? I thought that Nick could help us outline all our financial issues, you and I seem to be okay about the custody. What else do you want to discuss?"

"Ben, I think we have more going on here than just some property and custody issues. What about college for the kids? What about support for them until then? What about alimony for me? What about this house? What about my getting a job or going back for an advanced degree? There are probably some other issues I'm overlooking. Do you think we can resolve these by ourselves?"

"I'd like to give it a try before we start bringing other people into the picture. What does your attorney have to say about this?"

"Morgan has *Divorce with Dignity in* her waiting room and encouraged me to read it. I asked her about mediation and she recommended I read that step before advising me further. She said she knows someone we could use if we decide to go that route."

"I'm all for resolving this amicably, but I think you and I should try talking about these things first and then run our decisions by our lawyers. If we can't get something done, let's think about a mediator then. Okay? Do you think we can do this?"

"I'm game if you're game. As long as everything we discuss can be reviewed by counsel.." Samantha's uncertainty about negotiating one-on-one crept into her voice. "Absolutely. When do you want to start?"

"Why not now?"

With that the couple began their first negotiating session, discussing their concerns for their property, their futures, and most importantly the kids. They agreed to consult Nick together to get a complete portfolio of their stocks, money market accounts, savings and insurance. They discussed the need for the children to remain in the house at least through high school. Ben was reluctant to concede that they needed the house until they were through with college, but was wiling to think about that. He also acknowledged that it would be some time before Samantha was able to get back into the job force, but that she should start doing something toward getting her career back on track.

They also looked at the upcoming holidays and agreed the children should spend Thanksgiving with Ben and his family and Christmas Day with Samantha. Samantha was finally able to take a trip to NYC for the Macy's Parade and to see the Radio City Music Hall Christmas show.

And Samantha would keep both dogs at the house.

Exhausted from the talk and the three Dewars she drank, Samantha went to bed, tired, happy and three Dewars over her limit. She couldn't wait to meet with Morgan and get an agreement together. She also couldn't wait for the science center trip in the morning. How was that whale film?

Chapter Eleven

Samantha awoke in the near dark. She smoothly slid into her morning stretches as her feet hit the carpet. The yoga and exercise routines were paying off as she no longer strained and groaned from the effort. Stretching done, she hit the shower, the hot water penetrating her somewhat tender muscles. Wanting to stay under the hot pulsating stream, she reluctantly got out, and toweled off. She walked over to her personal walk-in closet where she picked out one of her smarter outfits, a navy blazer, dark gray slacks and cream cashmere sweater. She added the Hermes scarf Ben gave her for Christmas last year. She knew she at least looked good for the day.

The weekend was over and Monday's agenda was meeting with Morgan, signed retainer and check in hand. She also had a copy of the document she and Ben had drafted containing all their agreements as well as the well those areas they disagreed on. She felt powerful and able to handle the challenges her lawyer and Ben's lawyer would be throwing at her. If only she didn't have some small doubts about their negotiated agreement. Had she done the right thing? Should she insist on a mediator? Why did she do this drinking Dewars? Was her judgement impaired? Would Morgan stop her from making a mistake? Would the internal questioning ever end? What she wasn't looking forward to was the backsliding the kids had done on the morning routine. Although they were getting themselves dressed and ready without a major confrontation, they were back to sleeping until Samantha invaded their rooms, waking them with her forced cheerfulness. Edward had returned to cocooning in his covers and Cynthia growled at her trespassing mom. But at least they were ready in time to enjoy a hot breakfast together before heading out the door.

Samantha gave air kisses to the kids as they entered the high school, aware their mother was unusually well-attired for the day, but blissfully ignorant of where she was going or what she was up to. Samantha rehearsed her speech to her attorney as she waited in the morning traffic, every car trying to violate the laws of physics by trying to fit into the same space. She ignored the potential cluster fuck that was avoided as more patient drivers waved through the impatient. She successfully focused on the cars ahead, pulling into the parking lot nearest Morgan's office with all the others.

She was only a few minutes early, having booked the first appointment of the day. This promised to be a lengthy appointment that would take until lunch time. Ben asked her to call him when it was over and had offered lunch. Samantha made no commitment, choosing instead to see how things worked out with her lawyer.

As before, Laurie welcomed her into the office, and offered her some Constant Comment tea that the smart receptionist remembered Samantha liked from her first appointment. Samantha was impressed by the friendliness and efficiency of her new lawyer's office. Laurie informed her that Morgan was on the phone but would be out shortly.

A few moments later, Morgan poked her head into the reception area and beckoned Samantha into her office. Once inside, Samantha girded herself for the conversation to follow, expecting objections from her lawyer to her personally negotiated agreement. What followed was a pleasant surprise.

"Ben and I met last week to work out the details of our agreement. We don't have everything resolved, but I think we made some real progress." Samantha blurted out her opening in a single breath, waiting for an objection from her lawyer.

"So you were able to talk to each other. How was that?" Morgan took the papers Samantha handed her and set them aside. "Did you feel comfortable?"

"Yes and no," Samantha replied as she poured some tea into her cup from the little pot Laurie produced. "I kept questioning whether we needed a mediator. But in the end, I felt pretty comfortable talking directly to Ben without someone else present. Maybe it was the Dewars talking, " Samantha admitted, a tad embarrassed.

"Did you read the step on mediation before this took place?"

"Yes, and I mentioned it to Ben who asked if I thought I could do this without a mediator. It's not that he rejected the idea out of hand, he just wanted to save a few bucks by not having another person involved."

"But you do understand the role of the mediator? Someone to level the playing field in case of some power imbalance?" Morgan's voice remained kind with just a hint of school teacher.

"Yes. But I understand Ben's viewpoint as well. There's just so much money to go around and we don't want to spend it on unnecessary things." Samantha's voice became just a tad defensive, wondering if she sounded like a major idiot to this woman.

"Well, there's nothing wrong with the parties speaking to each other without a third party, such as a mediator, present. I encourage my clients to do this all the time. I know divorce becomes expensive, especially when one party is paying the entire bill. I just want to make sure that you're comfortable with this arrangement, especially since he's a lawyer. Just make sure that he doesn't want to bring in his lawyer when I'm not there. And I hope he's clear that these agreements between the two of you have no effect until your lawyer reviews them and we set them down in a written document you both sign." Morgan laid out her rules of negotiating directly with the other party which suited Samantha fine.

"I believe we're agreed on that. I told him I was seeing you today to go over what we already agreed to and to discuss how next to proceed. By the way," Samantha reached into her handbag, "here's your retainer and signed fee agreement."

"Thanks," Morgan responded. "It's always nice when I don't have to lift up my client by their ankles and shake the check out of them," she joked.

"Well, what next?"

"How about waiting here while I read this document. Your handwriting?"

"Yes. If Ben wrote this it would be illegible."

"Nice handwriting. Catholic school?" Morgan asked.

"No, Mrs. Wilson, fourth grade, public school. She saw some potential in me and drilled me until I mastered this writing."

"Good work. I can't always make out what my clients scrawl. And you should see some of the judges' writings. You need a typed transcript to make out the orders they write." With that, Morgan turned her attention to the document and intensely read each word.

When she finished, she turned her attention back to Samantha. "This looks like a good start. I have a few questions and I see where we need to discuss some unresolved matters. First off, are you agreed that your financial planner should detail all your personal assets?"

"Yes. I trust Nick implicitly. With the exception of his questionable taste in attorneys, " Samantha thought of her encounter with Velli, "I think he has both our interests at heart."

"Good. Do you think he's aware of any retirement plans or life insurance your husband has?" Morgan began raising the issues Samantha needed her to raise.

"I don't know. I know Ben has a 401k at his law office, and I know that Nick has nothing to do with that. But I don't know what's in it, and I don't know if Nick knows."

"Okay. That should be your first question to Nick. Make sure he has all the assets. I'll give you a worksheet that I'm sure he's seen before from other attorneys. We need to know what retirement accounts exist, as well as any life insurance."

"Ben always claimed that he had plenty of insurance on himself so that the kids and I would be okay. In fact, his insurance is in a computer file marked "jic - Just in Case."

"Good. Make sure we know what type of insurance it is and what the beneficiary designation is. We want to make sure that if this is to continue to provide for you and the kids, the beneficiary designation is made irrevocable and that there's a sufficient amount to cover your living expenses, as well as the kids."

"For what duration? Forever?" Samantha had always been somewhat mystified by insurance and wasn't really sure what to ask for.

"Well, what are your concerns financially? You mentioned before you wanted to make sure the kids got through college. Graduate school is not a stretch, either, given the fact that your husband has a law degree. So we want to make sure there is a sufficient amount to take care of that until your youngest, Edward, is done with graduate school. Say age 25?"

"That sounds right. What about me?" Samantha was afraid that if something happened to Ben, she wouldn't be able to afford the house and all the incidentals involved with, well, life.

"Samantha, it's time for you and me to get real. What about you? What do you want to be doing after this divorce?" Morgan focused her full attention on Samantha, ready to start the career talk. Morgan reached for her tissues, ready for the waterworks.

"I've been thinking a lot about this lately. I don't feel ready to start back where I left off when Cynthia was born." Samantha thought about her former life working for a large department store as a buyer.

"What were you doing when Cynthia was born?"

"I was a housewares buyer for Janek's Department Store. When I was pregnant I quit. Now the store's no longer in existence and I haven't worked for the past seventeen years."

"Did you enjoy working as a buyer?"

That was the million dollar question. Samantha remembered complaining to Ben every night when she got home about the long hours, the vendors, the travel. She didn't see herself doing that again. "Not really. I really didn't like that job. But it was something to do while Ben got his law degree and started working."

Divorce with Dignity
Kathleen Berge Entenmann

"What do you see yourself doing?"

"Well, my degree is in English and I'm certified
to teach K-12. I always wanted to go back into the
classroom. But I haven't taught since my student
teaching. The only job in teaching I could get was
substitute teaching. I tried doing that when the kids were
little, but I often had to turn down jobs because someone
was sick or at home and I needed to be there. After a
while I just gave up." Samantha thought she sounded
defensive when answering a question about not working
when the kids were small. She started to fold her linen
napkin neatly.

"I know. It's impossible to feel you're doing a
good job raising your children when you have to work
full-time. You're lucky that you were able to stay home.
That's such an important job. Don't feel defensive for
being there for your kids; that's your first responsibility
when you're a mother. This superwoman, we can have
it all, I'm every woman, is so much crap. You wouldn't
believe the number of my colleagues who've stroked out
trying to have it all. Really. A few of them died and
some are now retired, trying to keep their blood pressure
under control."

"Really? I always thought I was a slacker for not working with the kids at home. Ben would sometimes mention that he thought I should go back to work and made me feel somewhat lazy for wanting to stay at home. But a stroke? Really?" Samantha felt that the current stress she was under was tough, but at least not life threatening. She tried a new folding pattern for her napkin.

"Sorry for that outburst. It just made me reevaluate my own life. Hence the trip to New Zealand. I really need time to relax and recharge. But back to you. Do you want to teach?"

"I think so. The trouble is there are really no jobs around here for English teachers. I thought about going back to school for my masters and maybe working as a TA there while getting my degree. While there I could work part-time at one of the technical schools that needs an English instructor. As long as you have your degree, they're really not picky."

"Sounds like you've put some thought into this. Have you looked into graduate programs and schools looking for instructors?"

`"A few. Larry, one of Ben's friends, teaches law at a school where they train future mall guards in their law enforcement program. He said the place is always in need of new instructors. I thought I'd apply for a job there."

"Sounds good. I like the idea of you getting back into the work force. It does two things: you're back on track with working and Ben can't say that you're not trying to contribute to the family."

"I have to admit, I'm a bit nervous about this. But I'll see what happens. Larry offered to set me up with an interview right away if I wanted. Apparently they're that desperate." Samantha tried a new napkin style, going for the difficult goose pattern her mother taught her.

"Well, good luck. I know it can be rough getting back into the swing of things, especially after a long lapse. You'll be great, though."

"I wish I were as confident as you." Samantha dropped her napkin and suddenly began crying, loud, hysterical sobs.

Morgan looked at her with mixed astonishment and sympathy. "Okay, I'm now about to say the most stupid thing you can to someone crying. Calm down."

Samantha blew her nose and kept crying. "See, it never works. Cry it out and we'll talk." Morgan sat in the other client chair beside Samantha, holding the tissues and occasionally offering the box to her out-of-control client.

After a few minutes Samantha's outburst stopped. Morgan listened to her last few sobs and offered Samantha a hug. "Better? I'm a little surprised. You've always seemed so confident and together. What happened?"

"Sorry about that. It just started crashing in on me. The divorce, the kids, the house, the future. I don't want to deal with any of it."

"No need to apologize. This is scary stuff. Frankly, I'd be even more distressed if you never had an outburst. People who are always in control sort of freak me out."

"Then you would have loved my grandmother. She apparently never had an outburst in her life. So German, always in control."

"Samantha, grief is real. It's expected. Your life has taken a dramatic turn. It's not going to be the way it was."

"I thought I was past this. I had a major meltdown in my friend's kitchen when this started. Since then I've been okay." Samantha surveyed the array of used tissues scattered about the floor and began picking them up. "This really caught me by surprise. Sorry."

"Look, Samantha, we could go ahead with a discussion of the settlement. But I don't think that's wise. Have you thought about seeing a counselor?"

"When I first talked about this with my friend Jordan she made that suggestion. I just didn't want to go see someone and talk about this. I still don't want to talk about this, even to you. No offense."

"None taken. I realize how difficult this is for clients. I don't take lightly what you're going through. I know it feels as though part of you is dying every time you come in here. It's why I try to settle these matters fairly and quickly so that you don't unduly suffer."

"Some of that transactional cost the book talks about." Samantha mentally patted herself for remembering the phrase.

"Exactly. But I can't do my job if you're not up to doing yours. I need you to advise me as much as you need me to advise you. If you're emotionally awol I can't do my job."

"I hear you. Is it okay since I'm here if we just go through one more thing. I'm really going to need your help with this."

"Sure. Tell me what's on your mind. Maybe I can ease your mind. Let me guess - the house?"

"Yes. Ben and I agree that the kids and I should remain there, but we can't agree on a time limit. He wants to sell the house when they're through high school and I want to wait until they're done with college." Samantha neatly laid out the argument for Morgan's consideration.

"Why the end of college?" Morgan was hearing a rather new proposal. She knew the law and most parties agreed to the end of high school.

"I just want them both to have a place to come home to during college. I want them to have their home, their bedrooms, their friends." Samantha explained her reasoning, her voice somewhat pleading.

"That sounds great, Samantha. But have you considered the financial burden that puts on both of you?"

Divorce with Dignity
Kathleen Berge Entenmann

"Me too?"

"Sure. As long as the house is unsold, you're both responsible for the mortgage. Plus you have upkeep on your part for an aging home. We're looking at the house being eight years older by the time your son is through college."

"What about Ben's responsibility for those expenses?" Samantha was grasping at straws, certain that she was losing this argument with her own lawyer. It wasn't a good feeling.

"Samantha, there are many things we can do with the house. You can both continue to own it and then sell it and divide the proceeds at an agreed upon time. One of you can have the title transferred to you alone. The problem with this is if you have title, you also should have responsibility for the mortgage. If it were Ben who took title to the house, no problem with the bank. I'm sure they'd be willing to refinance or recast the mortgage in his name. You - probably no.

That leaves us with the option of having you taking title and giving Ben an indemnification agreement. You'll pay the mortgage and if you default, you agree to take responsibility for any legal action. The problem with these agreements is that they're about as worthless as the subprime mortgages that led to the recession. If you can't afford to pay for the mortgage, how can you hold the other party harmless?" Morgan stopped to get her breath.

"So what do you think? Do you think Ben is right?" Samantha started sounding defensive again.

"What I think is that you both need to discuss this. I'll take our positions to Ben's lawyer, but you're telling me you two don't agree. If you feel comfortable talking to Ben, I'd suggest you do that. But first, I think you should seriously consider a therapist or counselor. I'm not sure you're thinking straight at the moment. This is too important a decision."

"But I don't want to see a shrink. I already explained that to my friend Jordan and she's the one who suggested I get a self-help book. Do you really think I need to talk to someone? Ugh." Samantha visibly grimaced and shook at the thought.

"What I think doesn't matter here, Samantha. This is your life. It's not my place to torture you through this process. I'm only suggesting what I think could make this easier."

"I appreciate that and I appreciate that you want me to help in the decision making. It's just that...that.. this is *so unfair.*" Samantha began crying again and Morgan passed her the tissues.

"I agree it's unfair. Life is unfair. Can you think of a way to make this *more* fair?"

"I just wish Ben had to suffer through this. No, that's not it. I just wish he were as inconvenienced as I am. That's it. He is an attorney, he knows attorneys, he has an attorney right in his office. He leaves our house and gets himself a nice condo. He gets to see the children whenever it's convenient for him. He starts all this and then I have to suffer. For both of us. He'll always have more money, more freedom. And I feel like the one holding the bag. I wish he had to see a shrink to get over this."

"Maybe he does. Maybe he needs to deal with this also. Do you think that he's really come through this undamaged? He obviously has issues that led to this in the first place."

"That's what I think. Most men get a sports car and get over their midlife crisis. He had to get a bimbo. Now he wants to uproot our lives. And from what I hear, he's not even with the same bimbo. He's out dating other women. Was I that unbearable?" Louder sobs followed the last question.

Morgan gave Samantha another hug. "I sincerely doubt it. But if you really want the answer to your questions, you'll have to ask him, not me. Here's a suggestion - how about couples counseling?"

"Isn't it a little late for that?" Samantha began to think Morgan was off her beam.

"Not necessarily to reconcile, but couples counseling to help with the divorce. Make it easier for both of you to accept what's happening. Have both of you air your issues in front of someone who can help you both understand what's happening to yourselves and to each other. Make this process easier to handle."

"Why is that any different than going to a mediator? Ben already said he didn't want to bring in third parties to this."

"Because this isn't what a mediator does. This is someone who's there to counsel you individually and together so that you stop suffering emotionally or at least can learn to handle the suffering. And you both may have some issues this person can help you with."

"I'll think about it. You may be on to something. I've avoided reading that step in the book so I guess I'll give it a read and think seriously about it." Samantha balled up the tissues and threw them in the trash basket across the room.

"That's all I can ask you to do. In the meantime, I'll draft a letter to Ben's attorney about what we believe to be the basis for an agreement and where we still have to work out issues. I'll send it to you first to make sure everything is correct. If you have a problem with anything, call the office so we can discuss changes. I want to make sure I fairly represent your position on everything." Morgan stood up, ending the meeting and gave Samantha another hug. "Think about a counselor..Seriously."

Samantha left the office, feeling somewhat unburdened and hopeful that serious negotiations were about to begin. She ducked into the nearby Macy's. wandering aimlessly, right into the cosmetics section. Several women approached her with perfume scented cards, hoping to allure Samantha over to their counters for an expensive purchase. The Estee Lauder saleswoman offered her a make over. Samantha mindlessly sat down, subjecting her face to the application of foundation, blush, eye shadow, mascara and lip liner. The cosmetician kept up a constant sales pitch about the products, Samantha occasionally answering her with a yes or nod of approval. When the makeover was finished, Samantha didn't recognize herself. It had been years since she applied cosmetics, usually just cleaning her face and putting on some moisturizer.

"Wow. That's me? It doesn't look like me." Samantha stared at her new face in the hand held mirror.

"Don't you like it? I think it brings out those beautiful hazel eyes. Your skin is fabulous - you must take great care of it." The saleswoman tried to save her commission.

"I'm just not use to this. I don't wear much makeup. I'm usually at home alone or running errands. But now that I'll be going back to work..." Samantha let her voice trail off, not wanting to begin another crying jag in front of a complete stranger.

"This routine is so easy for you to do each day. I promise within five minutes your face will be complete."

Divorce with Dignity
Kathleen Berge Entenmann

The saleswoman's voice rang with the promise of a resuscitated sale.

"Well, let me have what I need. I like this light base; it doesn't feel like the heavy greasepaint I wore as a kid. I'll need eye shadow and blush."

"Great. Let me get the product together and ring you up. Because of your purchase today, you'll get a free makeup bag and tote and a bottle of Private Collection." The saleswoman flitted about the counter, calculating her commission, hoping Samantha would become a regular customer. Samantha handed over her Macy's charge, vaguely aware of the total cost of the sale, and little concerned. The bills still went to Ben. Let him pay for her new face.

Shopping bag in hand, Samantha found a quiet corner in the shoe department where she eyed a new pair of heels. She sat in one of the chairs, pulled out her cell phone and called Ben.

"Sam. Are you done with your lawyer? Still want to have lunch?" Ben sounded relieved that Samantha called him.

"I'm over at Macy's where I just bought new makeup for my new career look. Right now I'm looking at shoes. But I'd rather have you buy me lunch than another pair of shoes I probably don't need." Samantha waved off a hovering salesman who had the same hungry look as the Estee Lauder rep.

"Okay. How about meeting me across the street at The Barrister. Say ten minutes?"

"Fine. See you there." Samantha tossed her phone in her handbag, gathered her purchases and her emotions and headed for the exit. She stepped out of the store and into the next phase of her divorce.

Chapter Twelve

Samantha awoke in the near dark. Disoriented and confused, she tried to piece together yesterday's events. She had started yesterday in harmony with her life, hopeful that she, her lawyer and Ben could organize a new beginning for her. She ended the day feeling everything was so discordant.

Lunch with Ben was pleasant enough until Samantha broached the topic of a couples' counselor.

"Why would I want to see a counselor?" Ben asked, sipping from his lunchtime martini.

"Don't you feel you have issues to work out? If not personally, issues involving this divorce, the end of our marriage, your relationship with the kids?" Samantha began buttering a crescent roll.

"I know this sounds like one of those marvelous ideas that every couple should do. But we're not every couple, Sam. I don't think I have issues. I know what I want and unfortunately it means a divorce. Sorry." Ben took a big gulp from the martini, waving the olive and plastic sword at the waiter to order another.

Divorce with Dignity
Kathleen Berge Entenmann

Samantha felt her face heat up and the tears wet the backs of her eyes. She took a bite from her buttered roll, dabbed her face, and then spoke. "I know you don't think you have issues. Unfortunately, I do. And most of them are you. You don't think you're being somewhat selfish in all this? You don't think breaking up our marriage is a problem for you? Well, what about me? What about the kids?" Samantha finished her roll and reached for her water glass. The thought of throwing it on Ben occurred to her. But her overwhelming sense of propriety, even when dealing with a jerk, kept the glass in her hand and safely back onto the table.

"I'm not denying that this has been rough for you. It hasn't exactly been easy for me either. Don't you think I want to be with the kids every night? Don't you think I hate being a weekend Dad?"

"Actually, no. Whatever prompted you to want this divorce is still in control of you. You can now act out all your adolescent fantasies about being single. You can go out on dates and have the single life I obviously deprived you of. I know you always blamed me for talking you into marriage and kids. I should have just let you go on and live la vida loca when we graduated from school. Sorry I ruined your life." Samantha pushed her chair back, ready to leave, her final words choked out in anger.

Ben stood up and reached across the table to grab Samantha's arm. "Don't go. This is not what I want. I don't want you to be angry with me."

Samantha took her free hand and removed Ben's grip on her arm. "Then stop *pissing me off.* You want a war, I'll give you war. Have a lovely lunch. Maybe you can call one of your bimbos to take my seat."

With that Samantha stormed to the cloakroom, got her coat and bags and headed out for the parking lot. She would pass her favorite gyro place on the way home and stop in for her version of comfort food. Gyros and fries could help her get through most upsets, including walking out of an expensive lunch with Ben. She needed a bag of good grease right now.

When she got home. she got a plate and set out her lunch. A glass of diet soda would have to do. She made it a policy never to drink alone during the day while the kids were at school. What if she had to go and get them unexpectedly? She heard stories about irresponsible mothers who liked to drown their misery during the day with wine or harder stuff. She wasn't about to join their ranks.

Samantha thought about her life as a mother. She always tried to do the right thing, even when it wasn't the convenient thing. Who made sure the kids were picked up from school, outings, movies, activities? Samantha. Who got the unwanted, burned, undercooked, overcooked food? Samantha. Who kept her wits about her when the kids were at school, at home, at friends? Samantha. Who coached basketball and soccer teams? Samantha. Samantha was always there, even when Ben was in the home. She was the one to make sure that everything ran smoothly. She was the one to make life easy for everyone. She was the one who made it easy for Ben to leave.

Her cell phone was ringing her special Ben ring. No way was she ready to talk to him. Let him stew. She'd had enough. Was she going nuts? Maybe she did need a counselor or therapist. What did the book have to say?

STEP EIGHT - HIRE A THERAPIST, IF

NECESSAY

Do you want analysis, compassion and psychological advice from someone so screwed up they became a lawyer?

So many people take up golf and quit after a few lessons once they realize that God never intended the human mind and body to have to concentrate on so many directives at one time, simply to move a stationary ball 200 yards with a club. However, once you've taken your lessons, testing the patience of yourself and instructor beyond all human endurance, you possess the necessary insights to move that ball while appearing athletic and proficient. This doesn't mean that every time you play you'll hit lofty iron shots that nestle next to the pin or screaming drives that bound down the middle of the fairway. You'll still hook, slice, skull, shank, and flat out miss the ball. But you now possess the insight, knowledge and conviction to make the necessary corrections. More importantly, you have the insight,

knowledge and conviction to know that you've played the

game with reasonable success and can do the same

tomorrow and on into the future.

Not everyone goes through life with the ability to

deal with its problems competently all or even part of the

time. We all need instructors at one time or another to

help us succeed. When we're young, that's our parents'

job; they guide us through the jungle of learning to walk

without falling, talk without stammering or eat without

slobbering. As we age, others take over those

responsibilities, especially if we lack the ability to master

certain skills. We also have changing needs and need the

help of relatives, siblings, teachers and coaches to help us

with those needs. As good a golfer as my father was, I

couldn't learn the game from him. It took the patience

of someone more in tune with me to finally teach me the

game. It also required my getting older and more

mature so that I could look at golf not as a battle of wills between my father and me, but a learning process that might take years until I reached proficiency. Golf then became a game I could enjoy playing with my dad once I acquired the necessary skills.

Unless you possess the incredible ability to master any subject by simply reading and applying a text, you've needed the help of others at times to help you master certain objectives, be it throwing a spiral pass, baking Tollhouse cookies or passing Calculus. Someone showed you, helped you, corrected you, counseled you, taught you, and guided you.

Frequently I am asked to resolve for clients what I call "life problems." These are very different from legal problems in that there is no legal solution. I feel as though I've raised a number of children because I've been asked parenting questions that are really not custody questions. I feel I've offered more advice than Dear Abby by commenting on relationship problems that cannot be resolved through a courtroom proceeding or pleading. I've been forced to tell clients they are wrong, wrong, wrong, when they make emotional decisions based on feelings, feelings, feelings.

I like to think of myself as a compassionate person and one who has a fundamental understanding of the human condition. But as savvy as I may be, I know that there are times when the problems of the mind and heart which bombard me across the telephone, internet or desk, are too complex for me to handle. I shudder to think that some people in acute crisis want me to solve problems that are completely outside my professional competency. These people need professional help other than mine.

I have a client I adore, not simply because he's a florist who sends me flowers with his payments, but who also has the insight to address certain concerns to me as "babysitting questions." These questions are generally in the nature of how he should react to a given situation - hang-up the phone, confront his ex-wife, take the children to therapy. These situations differ from a legal crisis that may require a snappy letter or pleading. He knows I am not a therapist, doesn't expect me to be one, but calls on my insights based on professional and personal experience. I truly appreciate the fact that he differentiates between my roles as attorney or counselor, and allows me to bail on a life question with an "I don't know what to do" answer.

For other clients, that line is not as apparent. I often feel the pressure of having to answer inquiries over problems that are probably best solved through the intake of psychotropic drugs. For me. Those clients are wasting their time and money by insisting that I listen to their complaints that are better aired on a psychologist's couch. But since they don't want to make the commitment to therapy after my numerous suggestions, they run up legal bills by soliciting my advice on matters I tell them are outside my expertise. They also stretch my patience by insisting on giving me problems I cannot handle. That lowers my self-esteem when I have to tell someone, "I just don't know."

Now is not the time to wander through the emotional morass of divorce by yourself, especially if you feel too lost or angry to deal effectively with life. Now is not the time to be macho and tough it out if you're not thinking clearly for yourself. Now is the time to seek professional help from someone other than your lawyer who is trained to listen to your pain and respond in a constructive fashion.

That said, let me begin by advising you that the therapist you choose is not going to have all the answers and cures for your pain. Not close. But given the opportunity, therapists can help with those feelings and hurts in order to get through this process with your self-esteem intact and perhaps even elevated.

To find this person, begin by asking your attorney for referrals. If your attorney's practice is focused on family law, numerous referrals have already been made. You are not the first client in need of this service. Chances are your attorney knows highly recommended therapists through former clients, colleagues, personal acquaintances or personal experience.

Once you've found the individual you're comfortable with, be as completely open and honest as you can be. This means first and foremost being honest about yourself, your strengths as well as your shortcomings. If you think you can walk into a therapist's office and lay blame for ll the sins of the world on your spouse, you are mistaken. Don't worry - your spouse's role in your current situation will be explored. But your own role in reaching this point is critical.

Why focus on your role when your spouse is the scum of the earth and architect of your misery? Because your therapist can only help you, not your spouse. You are the one on the couch, not your spouse. Unless your spouse agrees to go with you, the only player in this game is you.

If you are simply looking for sympathy and a shoulder to cry on, don't spend your money on a therapist. That's why you have friends and family who will listen to your bitching and bashing and tell you everything is going to be fine. Unfortunately, if you really want to make things fine, your friends and family may be clueless as to how to accomplish that.

Your therapist, on the other hand, is not there simply to listen to endless bitching and bashing. They're there to find out what's wrong with you, not your spouse, and to assist you in becoming a stronger person to deal with the complexities of this divorce and life after divorce. Your therapist is interested in what happened with your marriage from the standpoint of your role in the relationship and how to fix you. Again, you're the one on the couch, not your spouse.

Divorce with Dignity
Kathleen Berge Entenmann

One word of caution: clergy. While many members of the clergy are trained psychologists and counselors, many are not. Many also come into this area with their own agenda based on church teachings. This may not be helpful to you at this time, especially if you are uncomfortable with the church's position on divorce and the events that led to this juncture. Many clergy members do not share the life experiences of their congregations and are clueless as to what goes on on others' personal lives. Is this the person you want to take advice from in this matter?

Please do not take this as a complete rejection of religion and church. Turning to the church and personal faith can be an enormous comfort at this time. As a person of faith I do believe that the Almighty cares for us. He or She provides that care through many people, often those who are not robed and preaching to us from the front of the sanctuary. Be comforted by your religion and take your troubles to God in prayer. But if you are suffering, turn to a professional who can aid you in growing beyond the hurt.

One additional word of caution: friends and family. I earlier wrote how friends and family can be part of the problem and not the solution. Now may not be the time to expect that Mom or Dad or anyone close to you will have the best perspective on your life. Each of these people is heavily invested in your life and is too close to the problem to offer critical advice at this juncture. A good therapist will help you sort through the various issues objectively. A good therapist may also help you sort through the various issues you have with your friends and family that may have contributed to the demise of your marriage.

From my little window on the world I have found that in times of crisis there are generally three types of people. There are those who run for help at the slightest onset of psychic discomfort, hoping for either a quick fix or to engage in lengthy self-indulgent discussions with a captive audience. Then there are those who would love to run for help, but view doing this as a sign of weakness or who don't believe that anyone has the ability to help them through this acute pain. Finally, there are those who believe in the power of themselves, often with hard work, to reach mental health and peace with the help of others.

I don't believe in the power of others to cure my personal pain or provide my happiness. That's my job. But I do believe there are others who can assist me in that journey. Do you ask for directions from others when you're lost, clueless, mapless or your GPS directs you to the middle on nowhere? Do you continue to drive around aimlessly? I'm a woman; I ask for directions.

Therapist Checklist

- *Check with your attorney for referrals.*
- *Check with your closest friends for referrals.*

🌑 *Expect your therapist to provide guidance and support, but not an unlimited opportunity to dump on your spouse.*

🌑 *Be wary of clergy as therapists if their agenda does not match yours.*

🌑 *Don't use your attorney, friends or family as therapists.*

Tasks for step Eight

1. Have a serious conversation with yourself over your mental health. If the idea of talking out loud sounds insane, do it in your head. If you can't talk with yourself about the state of your emotional and mental health, speak with a friend or colleague who is able to observe your behavior and see whether or not you're handling life at this time.

2. Even if you and others think you're mentally and emotionally okay, consider making an appointment with a therapist for a mental "check-up." If you're concerned enough about your physical health to see a

physician yearly for a physical, then be concerned

enough about your mental health to see a therapist for

a "mental."

Samantha stopped reading and unclenched her

jaw. She didn't want this, but she knew from her

attorney's reaction and her restaurant melt down that

she probably wasn't handling life as well as she could.

Hell, even on her best days she felt that she was just

mailing it in. She was shocked that their public

appearance - the house, the kids, Samantha - hadn't

gone to hell. Everyday she awoke, she felt something

odd, something out of place. It now took her only a

second to remember that her life had become this

odyssey of living through divorce. She thought that was

progress; in the beginning it took her several moments to

become acclimated. Moments often accompanied by

tears.

She knew everyone was right. Even if Ben

didn't want to see a counselor with her, she needed to

go. Jordan pointed that out when she first saw her

months ago. Maybe Jordan would have a suggestion.

At least it was a place to start. She'd call her tomorrow and ask for a referral.

Samantha looked at her watch and realized it was time to leave to pick-up the kids. As she grabbed her coat and purse, she heard her cell phone ring from inside her purse. Ben's ring tone was playing. "Let him stew a while. I'll call him later." She left the house to get her kids and take them shopping for new winter coats and dinner. "I'll call Ben later with tell him about the latest charges on his Visa." Time for some retail therapy.

Chapter Twelve

Samantha awoke in the near dark. She could barely swing her legs out of bed. Her lethargy spread from her feet to her head, slowing every movement, delaying every action. "Screw the stretches," she mumbled, stumbling to the bathroom. I'll just hit the shower instead.

Samantha had dreaded this day since she made the therapist appointment last week. After speaking with Jordan she decided to take up Jordan on her suggestion and called Jonathan Travis. When Samantha reached the therapist by phone, she made it clear that she was not happy about the need to do this. The therapist chuckled in response.

"You're not alone. I don't see many people who are overjoyed at the prospect of seeing me. I guess I'm about as popular as a dentist."

"Don't get me wrong. I'm sure you're a very nice man and you sound like you have a sense of humor. But this isn't what I pictured myself doing." Samantha tried to defend herself.

Divorce with Dignity
Kathleen Berge Entenmann

"Don't feel bad, Samantha. I'd worry if you were thrilled to be coming in for an appointment. Most people aren't happy about this process. I'll see you Thursday at 11."

Today was Thursday and Samantha had to get the kids to school and then prepare herself for her first appointment. Yuck. She found the day ahead to be a trial to endure instead of a blessing to enjoy. In fact every day since she made the appointment had that feeling. The closer the day came, the deeper the dread, the greater the burden. Now it was here. Oh joy.

School days had an excited feel, that December-Christmas-is-coming-excitement. Teachers were doing their best to keep the students interested, but everyone, including the faculty, was just mailing it in. Cynthia and Edward were more interested in holiday concerts and friends' parties than school work. Samantha also thought they annually tested her love as a mother by trying her patience beyond all endurance. If she still came through with the presents, she must love them, even though Santa had them on his naughty list. Her kids had always been more difficult the closer it was to Christmas. Oy!

Today she would drop off the kids, go into the city after a quick visit with and pep talk from Jordan. They agreed to meet at Susan's cafe, another new coffee shop in town. The barista made the best vanilla-caramel latte and the pumpkin muffins were usually sold out by the end of rush hour. The cafe catered to the moms who dropped off their kids and then came in for morning coffee klatches.

Jordan was waiting for Samantha, a hot vanilla caramel latte and pumpkin muffin waiting for her. Jordan dipped her biscotti into the strong espresso she started drinking after her culinary tour of Tuscany. Samantha once tried the brew and couldn't understand her friend's taste in coffee. To each her own.

"Ready for your appointment?" Jordan took a tiny sip from her demitasse.

"As ready as I'll ever be. Do I have to do this?" Samantha took a big bite from her muffin, powdered sugar dusting her face. She reached for a napkin.

"Yes, you have to put on your big girl pants and go see Jonathan. I'm sure it's not going to be as bad as you think. In fact you might enjoy it. Jonathan's a nice guy and I always found him easy to talk to." Another biscotti dunk.

"Do you mind telling me how you know this man? You've been pretty closed mouth about why you think so highly of this guy."

"Okay, I didn't want to make this public knowledge. A few years ago Greg and I were having some problems. I wasn't handling the situation too well. I felt I should talk to someone about what was going on, get some perspective you know. I remembered Jonathan from college and gave him a call." Jordan finished her biscotti, indicating her discussion of this topic was over.

"I'm sorry...I didn't know. Everything okay now? You want to talk?" Samantha stopped playing with her muffin and focused on her friend.

"Everything's fine. We had a few joint sessions and some individual sessions and learned a few things about ourselves and each other. But I'm not the patient here - you are. Stop deflecting. I'm more concerned about you right now." Jordan sipped her espresso, waiting for Samantha to respond.

"I wish I had known about this earlier. Maybe Ben and I wouldn't be in the shitter. You and Greg are fine and Ben and I are apart."

"Would you have recognized that anything was wrong with your marriage? Were you fighting? Were you not speaking to each other? Did you know about the affair? What did you know?"

"Nothing. I was blind to what was going on. All I cared about was getting through each day with the kids. I didn't pay attention to Ben. I didn't see this coming." Samantha's voice started choking up, the initial wounds opened again.

"Then stop blaming yourself for not going to a therapist earlier. You thought everything was okay. We all thought everything was okay. If your friends didn't see this coming, how could you have? But this is something Jonathan is going to ask you about. Just be prepared. And it's okay to cry. He's not one of those men who can't stand tears. It's an occupational hazard with him." Jordan reached into her purse and pulled out a new pocket sized pack of tissues. "Just in case he's out."

"Thanks. I do believe I'll be needing these. And I don't rely on the kindness of strangers, so I'm not betting on Jonathan having enough for my waterworks."

"Just try to relax. I really think you're going to like him. You two seem to have the same sense of humor and appreciation for literary allusions."

"Ooh, allusions. Someone's been helping her kids with their homework."

"Just SAT words. We're hoping for better than a 500 on the verbal part."

"Well, if you need help with that, give me a call. I helped coach Cynthia to a 680 on her verbals in the PSAT."

"That's because your kids are, what do you call it, smart. Mine are television and video junkies who wouldn't pick up a book outside of school on a bet."

"Don't be so harsh. They'll surprise you yet."

"I'll believe that when the acceptances start pouring in. Right now it's looking like community college, and that might be a struggle."

"Well, give everyone a hug for me. I'm off for some pre-therapy retail therapy followed by my first session of torture."

"Would you stop thinking of this as torture? I think you're going to feel much better afterwards."

"Thanks. Ta ta." Samantha reached over and hugged Jordan. She actually felt better about the upcoming session and started to focus on the positive that could come of all the talking and crying. Maybe she could start feeling better all the time after this. Nah.

Samantha managed to avoid the majority of the rush hour traffic into the city. She parked and decided to wander about, checking out the holiday decorations and store windows. The windows she had always enjoyed were disappointing, looking as though some talented elementary school students had designed them. The Christmas tree in front of the county courthouse was huge as always. In what other city could they stop traffic all afternoon in order to put up a tree?

Samantha made her way to the therapist office. Jonathan Travis, Psychologist. "Let the games begin. God be merciful."

When Samantha entered she found no receptionist, just an empty waiting room with a coffee pot and overstuffed chairs to relax in. She took off her coat and folded it over one of the chairs since there was no coat rack or closet. She sat down and reached for a People magazine that promised the latest gossip about celebrities she neither knew nor cared about. Why wasn't there a Sexiest Man Alive issue?

Promptly at 11 Jonathan Travis appeared before her. His office connected directly to the waiting room. She noticed when she was inside that his office had two other doors, one that opened to a bathroom and the other an exit to the outside corridor. "I heard about this," Samantha remarked, pointing to the exterior door. "Your patients don't see each other coming and going. Nice."

"Privacy is an important concern. You never know who's going to be waiting or in here talking with me. I don't feel it's ethical to allow others to know who's receiving treatment. Not that there's anything wrong with that."

"Treatment or having the world know?"

"There's nothing wrong with receiving treatment. Unfortunately, the whole world doesn't share that view. What's your view on treatment? You sounded more than a little reluctant on the phone." Jonathan gave her an opening to start venting.

Divorce with Dignity
Kathleen Berge Entenmann

"To tell the truth, I've never been a big believer in therapy. I've always kidded my friend Jordan about psychobabble bullshit, just to get a reaction. But after the past few weeks, I've come to a point where I think I may need some help."

"What's been going on the past few weeks?"

"My husband and I are trying to finalize our divorce."

"Whose idea was the divorce? Are you separated? When did all this happen?" Jonathan shot her a series of questions that would require a lengthy explanation of the past few months.

"The divorce is my husband Ben's idea. He moved out a few months ago after announcing that he had been having an affair. I thought he might want to come home when he started coming over for dinners before the kids' events. But it turns out he still wants a divorce. I think he's having a midlife crisis, but he doesn't see it that way. I think he needs to see someone for help, but he doesn't see it that way. I think he's being horribly unfair to me and our kids, but he doesn't see it that way." Samantha angrily punctuated her statements with an audible grunt.

Divorce with Dignity
Kathleen Berge Entenmann

"Sounds like the two of you need to be here. But I can't put a gun to his head and insist he come see me. So we're going to focus on you and helping you deal with what you've already described as an unfair situation. So how did this start?" Jonathan leaned back and gave Samantha the floor to begin her story. By now she was pretty good at filling in all the details. It helped that she had to tell it to her attorney and related most of the facts to her friend, Jordan. She selectively edited the story for her family, filling them in on the details she felt willing to share. Admitting she was dumped for another woman was still something she was unwilling to relate.

"And I feel uncontrollably angry right now and I hate that feeling. I hate losing control." Samantha stopped and caught her breath.

"Everyone hates that feeling. What do you do when it happens?"

"Mainly, I cry. I'm so worked up that I can't express myself and I just start bawling. That's the worst part of this." Samantha grabbed for a tissue and began dabbing her eyes.

Divorce with Dignity
Kathleen Berge Entenmann

"Are the emotional outbursts more frequent now?" Jonathan tried to gauge how distraught Samantha was.

"Yes. I think of all the things I have to do now and I just feel like giving up. I'm tired and I just want to either cry, sleep or hit something." Samantha sighed.

"You said you think of all the things you now have to do. Are these things part of the divorce?"

"Yes and more."

"Such as?"

"Well, I realized the other day that I have to be the responsible adult. I mean I always have been, but now I have to be ready at all times"

"For?"

"Mainly for the kids. In the past, I've always taken care of the kids, made sure they were taken to where they had to go and picked up afterwards. I've always been there when they were sick or had homework or the occasional incident."

"Incident?"

"Oh, a few run-ins at school requiring detention or conferences with teachers. Nothing major, just stuff that happens. I'm always the one to go to the school and take care of things."

"And this has changed how?"

"Well, on a few occasions, I could count on Ben to step in and help. If I was under the weather, he'd take over the kids. But now he won't be there and I'll have to do this by myself."

"You don't think he'd help out if you called him?"

"He's always so busy. By the time he returns my phone call the crisis has past and I've worked it out." Samantha sounded slightly bitter.

"Has there ever been a time when something dire happened and no one was able to respond? Have you ever stranded your kids or not gotten them medical attention?"

"No. I sometimes call my friend Jordan to help out. She's picked them up from school on a few occasions. And we both use the same pediatrician so she knows where to go in a medical emergency."

"So you've worked out a plan with Jordan in the case of some rare emergencies. The kids sound like they're being taken care of. What else is going on?'

Jonathan continued to patently cross-examine Samantha.

"There's house stuff. I'm really pretty handy around the house, but Ben takes care of most of the small repairs."

"Such as?"

"Replacing the light bulbs in the overhead fixtures. Cleaning the furnace filter."

"Have you tried to do these things?"

"No, but I think I can. I'm probably more adept at using a screwdriver, hammer and drill."

"Okay. Is there anything else?"

"Well, Ben handles all the finances. I spend money and he pays the bills."

"Do you think you can learn to do that for yourself?"

"Well, I have a checking account I know how to balance. And our friend is a financial planner, so he knows about investments. Ben always took care of the income taxes."

"Does he do them himself?"

"No, we have an accountant."

Divorce with Dignity
Kathleen Berge Entenmann

"Do you think you can use the accountant as well?"

"Yes. It's just something I don't want to deal with."

"Join the club. No one in their right mind wants to deal with taxes. It takes a special person to want to do taxes. The normal person doesn't want to go there." Jonathan had a cathartic moment. Thoughts of his parents wanting him to get an accounting degree danced through his head.

"I guess I just really don't like the thought of dealing with anything. It's not that I can't do this stuff, I just don't want to have to do this stuff. At times it just seems, well..."

"Overwhelming? An unbelievable pain in the ass? Unfair?" Jonathan filled in Samantha's emotions.

"All of the above. Why me?" Samantha whined.

"Do you seriously believe you can handle everything? If so, you're more than half way home in coping with this divorce. So many women, and some men, don't have a clue. But you appear competent and calm." Jonathan tried to reassure Samantha.

Divorce with Dignity
Kathleen Berge Entenmann

"But I'm freaking out on the inside." Samantha
tried to talk herself into a nervous breakdown.

"I don't doubt that. But if you think you're not
handling this right, let me assure you that you seem
more in control than most. I have clients who do nothing
but cry morning to night. I have clients who can't do
anything without outside assistance. I had a woman
who had to hire a plumber to plunge the toilet because
she had never done it. Nothing complicated. But there
are people out there who are clueless. I know men who
always have to eat out because cooking anything more
complicated than a peanut butter sandwich is beyond
them. And these people all wonder why they're broke."
Jonathan took a breath after his diatribe.

"It's not that I can't take care of the ordinary
stuff. I just chose not to once I got married. That was
the deal. I handle the kids and the housekeeping and
Ben does the yard work and minor repairs. He always
dealt with the finances. I didn't have to do to that stuff. I
really, *really* resent having to deal with it now."
Samantha stopped as she felt the tears coming out. She
gave a loud sniffle and composed herself.

"Will being angry get any of this done? Is your anger going to stop this divorce? Does it make you feel better?" Jonathan stared at Samantha, waiting for an answer or another tirade.

"No. I have to do these things. I can't stop the divorce. And being angry does not make me feel better. My blood pressure is up and my stomach hurts. I feel like shit."

"I think I know how to make you feel less shitty. Start taking care of your life and stop resenting your husband."

"Easier said than done."

"Without a doubt. Trust me, the sooner you stop resenting your husband for putting you in this position, the better you're going to feel."

"Really?"

"I'm so sure that we're not going to schedule another appointment right now. We'll wait until you've started doing these things for yourself. If you don't feel better then, the next appointment is on me."

"A guarantee? Are you kidding?" Samantha found the offer exceedingly strange.

"I think I understand human nature and can judge character. I think this has been just a check-up. You needed to vent and get some instructions. You're strong and you're going to be fine."

"From your lips to God's ears." Samantha smiled and gathered her things.

"I know from whence I speak. Be strong. Take care of yourself." Jonathan reached over and gave Samantha a parting hug, holding her a bit longer than he usually would.

"Thanks. I'll take your advice. The book I'm reading suggests becoming more independent, now that I'm on my own. You've added weight to that advice."

"Samantha, call me if you need me. But I really believe that things will work out for you. Besides, you don't need a large therapy bill on top of your other expenses."

"Is that in your best interests? Don't you need clients to make a living?"

"Of course. But believe me, I have plenty of people in worse shape than you. I won't starve," Jonathan added ruefully.

"Well, goodbye. Thanks for the ear and the advice."

"Remember to call me if necessary. Or just to update me. I really enjoyed meeting you. Things will work out. Trust yourself." Jonathan ushered Samantha out his exit door, closing it behind her as he went to the reception room for his next appointment.

When Samantha left she drove to the kids' school and waited for them outside. She wanted to take them home so they could finish their homework before going out with their Dad.

While she waited, she reread the independence chapter of *Divorce with Dignity*. It helped to reinforce the advice she just received from her new therapist.

STEP NINE - LEARN TO BE INDEPENDENT

There is nothing like being able to care for yourself to elevate your self-esteem.

A close friend of mine and longtime practitioner in New Jersey was advising me when I declared after college that I wanted to become a lawyer. At the time I had just graduated from Rutgers, completed my student teaching as an English major, and for reasons that surpass understanding decided to become a lawyer. My

friend was excited by my decision, if not my choice of

law school, and proceeded to tell me about practicing

law. Although I don't remember much about his

remarks, I do remember one thing: don't do divorce

work. Clearly, I listened closely to his advice.

According to my friend, the problem with

divorce work is that you get women clients who have

never changed a light bulb before and they're calling you

at 11 p.m. because the front porch light is out and the

burglars are surely going to invade her home. Forget

that you're the lawyer who's job is to resolve the legal

aspects of the divorce. You are looked upon as a source

of comfort and strength during times of stress, and that

extends to and includes an 11 p.m. phone call about a

burned out light on the front porch.

Happy to say this was never my experience. I

haven't been called upon to help change light bulbs for

my suddenly single women clients or dirty diapers for my

suddenly hands-on father clients. I steadfastly refuse to

offer my services in this area except to point out that all

the services you need domestically you can find online, in

a phone directory or by calling Mom or Dad. However,

as I earlier stated, I have been asked for relationship

and/or parenting advice from nearly every client. I have

offered my wisdom and guidance to help these people

become better ex-spouses and parents. I hope that I

have helped people learn to deal with problems in a

more adult and humane manner.

      I think it's time for another pop quiz to see how

capable you are to survive in this world on your own:

1. The following tools can be found in my house:

a. Hammer

b. Screw driver

c. Wrench

d. Pliers

e. All of the above

f. None of the above

g. Just duct tape - it fixes everything!

2. During an electrical storm the lights go out and I

a. Curse the darkness

b. Light every candle I own

c. Reach for a flashlight, only to find that the batteries are dead

d. Reach for a flashlight, confident that there are fresh batteries because I routinely change them

e. Call my mommy

3. A well balanced meal consists of:

a. All the foods on the food pyramid in their recommended proportions

b. Chocolate

c. Beer and anything else

d. Whipped cream and hollandaise sauce - everything else is just a base for these two foods

4. The most important thing to remember about doing laundry is:

a. Sorting the clothes according to fabric and color

b. Making sure to check all the pockets before washing

c. Making sure the dryer is set to the right temperature and time

d. All of the above

e. None of the above - just make sure you have someone to do your laundry for you.

5. My view towards personal finances can be best summarized as:

a. A penny saved is a penny earned

b. Use credit cards only in lieu of cash and pay off the balances monthly

c. Make an annual contribution to a retirement account

d. All of the above

e. I can't be out of money because I still have checks and if I play around with my credit cards I can squeeze some more money out of them.

If you answered e,d,a,d,d to these five questions, chances are you can make it through life without the intervention of professionals, friends or your mommy to

Divorce with Dignity
Kathleen Berge Entenmann

keep you fed, clothed and sheltered. If you answered

f,a,c, e, e you need crash courses on basic survival. By

the way, question 3 can also be answered b or d since

dark chocolate has been found to have many beneficial

qualities as a stress reliever and beta blocker. I also think

that most food is a base for whipped cream or

hollandaise sauce. Just don't make a diet of either.

If you have no experience as a domestic

engineer (cooking, cleaning, laundry, repairs) or a

business financier (balancing checking accounts,

budgeting household accounts, investing in retirement

accounts) learn to do so now. While at first your friends

and family may be eager to assist you, that enthusiasm

may not last long. Maybe the first summer of your

divorce your big brother will come out and help you

prune those trees and get the house in shape; by next

summer he expects you'll do this yourself. Maybe the

first few months of your divorce, Mom will cook and

clean for you; pretty soon she's going to tire of the

additional domestic chores thrust upon her and expect you to do it yourself or hire a maid. There's just so much good will out there. After listening to your tales of woe and now delivering on domestic chores, your friends and family will expect you to get on with life by yourself.

With this new found ability to perform tasks formerly outside the assigned roles in the marriage, comes a pride in realizing that life will go on. You are far more competent than you gave yourself credit for. From this feeling flows self respect that comes from the dignity of dealing with life after divorce. No longer do you have to store a list of numbers to speed dial in the event of emergency. Instead, you have a fully equipped tool box and basic knowledge of home repair. You have a fully stocked pantry, refrigerator and kitchen. You can cook, you can clean and you can repair. You are a self-sufficient person, worthy of admiration.

While you may learn to care for your basic needs, there is another area of your life for which you need to be responsible - being alone. Many newly separated people fail miserably at this. Some of us simply have to learn how to be alone without the companionship or distraction of others. If we cannot learn this valuable lesson, we become emotional cripples relying on the kindness of our children, friends and family for constant support and company.

I am convinced that this is why so many people have difficulty relinquishing any custody of their children to the other parent. Without the children around as a constant distraction, they have no clue what to do with themselves. Their sole definition of themselves is as a mother or father with the responsibility of feeding and cleaning up after children, taxiing them around to games and events, playing with and disciplining them on a constant basis. They don't realize how much noise the kids make in the house until the noise ceases when the other parent takes them out for the evening or overnight.

Divorce with Dignity
Kathleen Berge Entenmann

They have no vision of a day, much less a weekend or week, without being the nonstop parent.

But whether you have to adjust to spending time outside your role as parent, or outside your role as the better half of a couple, you will adjust and discover some pretty terrific things. Amazingly, being alone can be a liberating experience. While I do not minimize the pain of suddenly being without your children or rambling through a house you shared with someone else, you will find, over time, that time to yourself is something to prize, not shun. Suddenly it's not a battle for control of the remote; the entire cable system is your domain. It's not a question of whose taste in music prevails; rock out to all the jazz, classical, standards, new age, blues or rock you like. No one's there to object. At last there's time to just sit and be, to contemplate life or read in peace. The possibilities are endless. Don't allow the lack of a companion to keep you from doing all the things you've always wanted to do. Take advantage of the opportunity to get to know you.

One of the greatest discoveries I made about myself was that I still enjoyed playing piano. When my kids were toddlers, they refused to let me sit at the piano by myself and play. Worse still, if left alone in the room with me, they would start exploring underneath the grand piano whose stability I did not trust 100%. They always had to assist me by hitting the last few keys on the keyboard, whether or not they fit into the melody. I couldn't concentrate and in frustration stopped trying to master pieces I formally played with some proficiency.

Once they were with their father for weekends, I could sit at my piano and play whatever I chose. I could attempt to play Brubeck or Beethoven. I could practice as I needed to practice, endlessly going over difficult passages, trying to get my fingers to hit the correct keys in the correct order in the correct rhythm. And since I love playing and enjoy hearing myself make beautiful music, I was more relaxed and less stressed by the fact that the two people I love more than anyone weren't with me at that moment. I discovered I actually enjoy being alone, a good lesson to learn now that both of them are adults living away from me.

I've had clients whom I'm sure can't be alone for a single moment. If they call and and I can't interrupt what I'm doing to speak with them at that moment, they immediately make another call to someone else to discuss their latest tragedy. I know because my return calls are picked up by their voice mail. Their phones are constantly busy. Their work places are constantly filled with their tales of domestic woe. Their friendships are constantly consumed with getting through the latest crisis. And so many revel in this role.

Please don't act this way. Think about the quality of your friendships after you've spent emotional capital on this divorce. Will your friends have more to spend on your next crisis or will you be palmed off on others you haven't already exhausted with your

problems? Even if you were the supportive friend during

another's divorce, lending an ear to talk off, a shoulder to

cry on , and advice to ignore (they do), don't expect

reciprocity. In all likelihood, you resented your role as

emotional caretaker and they resented having to put you

in that role.

Becoming independent also means learning to

be your own best friend, your own confidant, your own

companion. You may not like everything about yourself

and chances are your friends don't either, despite the

little lies they tell you. Learn to talk to yourself as you

would another. Learn to give yourself advice as you

would another. Learn to joke with yourself as you would

another. In this day and age of bluetooth, people will

just suspect you're talking to someone on the other end

of the phone instead of yourself.

If part of this independence means talking to

your God, by all means do so. It is in those still moments

of communicating with our Supreme Being that the small truths of life are revealed to us. We express our deepest pains, needs and sorrows, and in doing so often find an answer for surviving these pains. We can chart better lives with the help of a divine being that left to our own devices and those of our friends may languish in pain.

Learning to live without your spouse's help

Oftentimes during this process it is tempting to call on the spouse to come and remedy your problems. "I can't get the garbage disposal to work - can you come over and fix it?" "I can't locate the documents you said were on the desk - can you come over and find them?" Often spouses, whether from guilt or a desire to maintain close contact with you, will oblige.

Unless you are in a dire emergency and your spouse is the only person who can possibly assist you, don't ask. Show your spouse that you are able to function without them. Don't use a crisis as a convenient excuse to rekindle a relationship. This is not the time for

reenlistment or reconciliation simply because you can't

handle loneliness or crises by yourself. This behavior is

unacceptable and exhibits a total lack of self worth.

This sort of behavior, the contrived domestic emergency

requiring the spouse's help, is the type of contrived plot

that kept fueling the plot lines of bubbly 50's and 60's

romantic comedies; don't make it your reality.

Your spouse will begin to resent the intrusion as

much as friends and family. If there's any hope for you

two to maintain a decent relationship post divorce,

you're sucking out its life blood with your endless

requests. Perhaps the two of you should sit down

together and create a manual for running the house, or

trouble shooting problems with the electricity, plumbing,

appliances, bank accounts. If these solutions don't help,

resolve to contact professionals if necessary. Better to

pay a plumber with cash than your spouse with a loss of

self respect when the garbage disposal refuses to dispose garbage.

Your credo at this time in life should be "Solve the Problem." Whatever the problem is, however it manifests itself, find a solution and *carry it out yourself.* This message seems so basic and self-evident, yet I find it's one of the most daunting and difficult tasks that each person going through separation and divorce faces. But how you succeed at striving towards independence is also a measure of how you are perceived as a person with self esteem.

Learning to live with less

Part of becoming independent is also learning to live within your means, especially financially. Perhaps you always harbored dreams of living in a gorgeous home surrounded by a few acres; now is the time to think affordable condo. Perhaps you liked the luxury of a leased parking space and driving your luxury sedan to work daily; now may be the time to consider the wonders of public transportation. In many ways you should be considering how to live with less in your life.

Simply reducing the material possessions and luxuries in our lives does not mean holing up in an attic apartment with only cold water and no internet or cable. Now is not the time to retreat into a cave with only the barest of life's necessities. But it is the time to seriously readjust your thinking on what you do and don't need.

A large part of being independent is finding what makes you truly happy and not relying on material fixes or retail therapy to get you there. This is especially important if you don't have the financial wherewithal to provide for those material needs you desperately need. You cannot become independent if you have a financial dependency brought on by overuse and misuse of credit and money.

Questions to ask yourself in preparation for independence

1. Am I comfortable being alone? If not, what can I do to help myself?

2. Am I comfortable handling domestic chores? If not, what help do I need?

3. Am I comfortable with financial issues? If not, what information do I need?

4. Am I comfortable turning to people other than my spouse for help?

5. Am I comfortable living with less?

Tasks for Step Nine

1. Sit down with your spouse, a parent or friend and go over the mechanics of your house if you are unfamiliar with the operation of any appliance or system. Make an operations manual, if necessary, explaining basic use, maintenance and repair.

2. If you are weak in any area of self-maintenance (cooking, laundry, finances, etc.) speak with a friend or relative who can give you instruction in that area. Better yet, if you have the resources, take courses such as a cooking class or personal finance management seminar and gain insights from a professional.

Divorce with Dignity
Kathleen Berge Entenmann

Edward and Cynthia startled Samantha as they opened car doors and piled inside. Samantha shut her book as Cynthia immediately launched into her latest tale of Mrs. Wilson's English class and how they all snickered while discussing sexual repression, Mrs. Wilson's favorite literature theme. Edward looked at his sister in disgust, clearly uncomfortable with this conversation. His class was currently reading To Kill a Mockingbird which inspired him to begin thinking about the law as a career.

"Homework?" Samantha asked, already knowing the answer. "How about a quick shopping trip before we head home. The two of you have been complaining about your sneakers."

"Running shoes, Mom. No one says sneakers. I *need* to buy some new running shoes for gym class. My old ones are falling apart." Cynthia made her shoes sound pathetic when in fact Samantha knew her daughter no longer cared for the style and color.

"Cool, Mom. I need new Nikes for school, too." Edward never wanted to be left out of a shopping trip, especially one to an athletic store.

"Fine. I think some retail therapy is in order for all of us. Let's do it."

Dick's Sporting Goods was nearby and Samantha wondered if the kids would be able to find shoes without trying on every pair in the store. Surprisingly Cynthia was not as fussy as Samantha feared in picking out a new pair of Adidas. She seemed to know exactly what she wanted and the pair the clerk tried on turned out to be her choice. Edward was somewhat more discerning, not wild about some of the color choices and styles. After trying on five pairs, he settled on one, different and somewhat more sophisticated than his current shoes. For whatever reason, the style of athletic shoe mattered even more than the clothes.

Samantha decided to get a pair for herself, thinking that the time had come for her to start a serious exercise program. Right after Edward was born she worked out to videos, not wanting to leave the house for a crowded gym. When Edward napped she was in the family room, huffing and puffing, listening to the baby monitor for the slightest excuse to abandon the exercise and attend to her son. Fortunately for her heath, Edward

slept through her sessions and her baby fat was soon
gone.

She stayed in shape, mainly through good diet
and long walks with the dogs. But the time had come for
her to start reconnecting with people. Jordan had been
trying to get her to join her gym for years, but Samantha
always had an excuse, bad memories of high school
gym class flashing whenever the suggestion was made.
Now joining a gym seemed to be a good idea for her to
combine a new social life with a healthy lifestyle. Getting
out in the world, leaving the comfort zone of home had to
be part of her new life after divorce. Maybe an Italian
cooking class would be next, giving her something to
work off in her new exercise class.

When they got home, the kids took their new
purchases up to their rooms along with their homework.
Samantha had barely taken out her shoes, laced them
and put them on when both kids were back down,
wearing the new shoes, ready to go out with their dad.
Samantha was skeptical that any homework was done,
but Cynthia and Edward assured her they had very little
and had finished what they had.

Soon Ben was at the door. Samantha decided to invite him in, something she hadn't done since the lunchtime restaurant scene.

"Hi. How're you doing?" Ben appeared somewhat shocked to see Samantha.

"Fine. I wanted to ask you a favor."

"Shoot. What do you need?"

"I would really like to get together to go over some things with the house and our banking so I know what goes on around here."

"Do you want to do this when I bring the kids back? Or do you think we need some more time?"

"I think we can handle it tonight, if you don't have plans. I'd really like to be able to take care of everything around here."

"Sure, no problem. I'll see you after the kids and I have dinner. Want to join us?" Ben was unnaturally generous, perhaps a bit remorseful over their last encounter.

The thought of going out again was not that appealing to Samantha. Was now the time to assert her independence, to purposefully choose loneliness over a dinner with her family? What would the book say? Screw the book, it's a free meal.

"Thanks. Let me get my coat." Samantha went to the hall closet.

"Mom's coming? Great." Cynthia's voice was a tad too enthusiastic, worrying both Ben and Samantha.

"It's just dinner, guys. Your mom and I have house business to sort out afterwards." Ben immediately stepped in to quell any unrealistic expectations from the kids. Were they ever going to stop hoping for a reconciliation?

"Okay, I'm ready. Let's go." Samantha used her mother business voice to get everyone moving.

"Where to?" Ben still didn't like making plans.

"Friday's. I love the hamburgers." Edward was all about the beed.

"Friday's is fine. I can get a salad." Cynthia was all about healthy eating.

"Samantha - you okay with this?" Ben seemed anxious to please everyone.

"Friday's is fine."

"Then let's go troops." Ben assumed the command position now that the decision was made.

Dinner was a complete pig out for everyone. Ben and Edward dug into fried cheese, wings, and potato skins for an appetizer while Cynthia and Samantha munched on the celery sticks. Hamburgers, steaks and salads were followed by desserts. Everyone groaned as they left the table. Samantha was afraid she wouldn't be able to stay awake to discuss business with Ben.

When they got home, Cynthia and Edward kissed both parents and went to their rooms. Samantha reminded them about their homework, skeptical that it was actually completed before Ben's arrival. She and Ben then went into the den where Ben assumed his familiar position behind the desk. As Samantha sat in the arm chair across the room, Ben looked at her sheepishly.

"I probably shouldn't be sitting here. Force of habit." Ben began to rise from the desk chair, offering it to Samantha.

"No, it's okay. Besides all the documents we need are in that desk and you're the one who knows where they are." Samantha waved Ben back into the chair, secretly pleased that he knew he was taking liberties in their current situation.

"Well, where do you want to begin? Finances?"

"Sure. We should be going through that stuff in order to get this divorce finalized."

"Most of our stuff is with Nick and I've asked him to get together a couple of files for each of us that show the investments and their current values. Your lawyer already requested this information and she should have it by the middle of next week. You know about our joint checking which I thought we should keep open so that I can deposit funds and you can have immediate access to them without having to wait for my check and then going to the bank."

"Do you really think that's such a great idea? What if one of us wants to clean it out?"

"Sam, I think that given our history that's not going to happen. Why don't you talk it over with your lawyer and give me an alternative if you still don't like that."

"I just thought everything would be separated out and we'd have no joint accounts or assets anymore."

Divorce with Dignity
Kathleen Berge Entenmann

"I think until we do something with this house,
we'll always have joint assets. And I don't know that this
is the time to start playing around with our investments
to separate them out. But if you want to, we can close
the joint checking and continue to use our separate
accounts." Ben managed to get through his statement
without his usual patronizing tone. Samantha was
impressed; maybe they could work out a settlement
together.

"Well, let me think about that. You make a good
point. As long as the two of us can trust each other,
maybe we can keep a joint checking account. I just
thought that you would want to move on, separate out as
much stuff as you could, start a new life without me in
the picture." Samantha started to tear up as she pitied
herself and by extension, her kids.

"Sam, you need to know that what I want is for
you and the kids to be okay. I've been a tremendous
asshole and I've done some incredibly stupid and
thoughtless things. I don't expect you to forgive me, but
I want to tell you I'm sorry. I want us to work things out
so that you and the kids will be okay. I want to be able
to have them continue to respect me and they can't do

that if they feel I've been unfair to you and them. So what do you say... can we work things out?"

"Yes, Ben. I do believe that's possible. But I want you to know right now, there's one thing I'm not compromising over."

"What's that?" Ben was worried that the new peace they formed was about to shatter.

"I insist on keeping the rattan elephant table." Samantha laughed, happy to see she had rattled him a bit.

"It's yours. Now let's get on with it. How about some coffee?"

"You know where the kitchen is."

STEP TEN - BE WILLING TO CHANGE

Facing your imperfections and working to improve them displays your continuing sense of self worth

"Where there is life, there is hope." I love this saying and I look to it when reinventing my life as circumstances change. No matter the current state of affairs, there is always the possibility of changing as long as there is life.

One of the people who has greatly influenced me is my brother who is thirteen years older than me. Alright, twelve and a half years. Most of my childhood was spent admiring his athletic prowess, be it swimming, football or basketball. He tirelessly taught me these sports and after high school my brother attended college to major in physical education. Unfortunately, my brother enjoyed life a little too much back then to be a serious student and ending up leaving after a brief stay.

Divorce with Dignity
Kathleen Berge Entenmann

After spending some time working in the private sector, my brother was invited by Uncle Sam to join the army. When he was honorably discharged, he met and married my sister-in-law who was an elementary school teacher. She helped convince my brother to return to college and after completing his associate's degree at the local community college, he went on to obtain a bachelor's degree at one of the nearby state colleges. Both he and my sister-in-law continued to teach until retirement a few years ago.

I teach part time at the local mortuary school where we have a number of non-traditional students, people who pursued other careers or raised families before coming to our institution. They range in age from their thirties to fifties. Some of them come to our school in order to become licensed to take over the family business that their husbands ran. Others just want a new career path and find this profession interesting. Still others seem to be floundering about, trying on new job titles as others try on clothes.

Whatever their reasons, they have not stayed stuck in a

job or profession they find unrewarding. They have

signed on for a new challenge.

Often with these new challenges come personal

upheaval. I have listened to the stories of some students

who are going through divorce, oftentimes struggling

with both a new career and a new lifestyle. Many of

them have children who also have to adjust to Mom or

Dad going to school, being away from home, pleading

for quiet so they can study for their next test. Theirs is

not an easy road, complicated by life and choices that

often were not of their making. I admire their

determination and dedication to get through a tough

curriculum. Oftentimes their road seems roughened by

the fact that they are not fresh out of school and are out

of the study habit. Oftentimes their road is easier

because they bring a determination and life experience

that other students don't enjoy.

Divorce with Dignity
Kathleen Berge Entenmann

Whenever I feel that I'm getting too old and set in my ways to change course, I think of my brother going back to school in his late twenties, married and with a child. I also think of these non-traditional students pursuing a new path in their lives. These examples give me hope. As long as we're breathing we still have the opportunity to change ourselves in so many ways.

This divorce is obviously a time of enormous change, one that you probably never thought you'd have to go through. But if you approached marriage with the knowledge that the odds were against you staying married to the same person until death do you part, you knew this was coming. If you didn't prepare for this life experience, now is the time where you will have to learn to adapt to the life changes you'll be going through. By now I would think that in the home economics courses there would be some mention of divorce along with teaching parenting responsibility by having students take care of a diapered flour sack or baby doll. But they don't

and so the lesson has to be learned the hard way.

Each and every divorce has a life of its own, a

rhythm, a growth and a conclusion. It is an organic

process that's not the same for every person going

through it. Your divorce may be rife with conflict over

property issues, while another's may be filled with

anguish over a custody dispute. Yours may end suddenly

with a well-thought out settlement proposal while others

may drag on for years, through the court and through

the lawyers.

While your divorce is being litigated or mediated

or conciliated or arbitrated, your positions will change.

You'll find it may not be worth $250 an hour in attorney

fees to fight over every stick of furniture in the house.

You can live with the children spending an extra night or

two every month with the other parent. You can afford

the extra $250 monthly to settle a support or alimony

claim. The absolutes you vowed you would never stray

from are no longer so absolute since you are now a participant in a conflict you desperately wish would end.

The point is, you will have to change, like it or not. A judge with the harsh comment to your attorney during a conciliation "tell your client that while I'm not deciding the case today, if I were I would not give him/her what he/she wants..." can change your mind in hurry. Counting the gray hairs or tracing your hair loss in the mirror each morning can change your mind in a hurry. Watching the pain on your children's faces as they hear you make another derogatory comment about their other parent can make you change your mind in a hurry. Suddenly things are no longer so black and white or worth the good fight you started out fighting.

Divorce will open your eyes to what your life has been and has become in a way that will not flatter or please you. You will examine and reexamine what your marriage was, what mistakes were made, how you could have avoided or corrected them. Your waking moments will be full of "woulduvs, coulduvs, shoulduvs." You will

vacillate from believing that divorce is the wisest move

you could have made and what took you so long to do

this, to divorce is the stupidest thing I could have done to

myself. You will experience every human emotion from

anger, depression, and uncertainty to acceptance,

elation, and contentment. Your friends will begin to

wonder if you are on mood altering medication.

Don't close down those feelings at this time.

While I wouldn't advise you to govern your life by your

current mood, I would advise you not to ignore these

feelings and to allow yourself to express them and

experience them. That doesn't mean, by the way, that

you go around like a fool asking friends and family to

"feel your pain" or by breaking into drunken fits of "I

love you, man." But be open to what's happening to

you. It will be the basis for learning to survive later.

I often joke that after going through childbirth

twice with only a shot of Demerol each time, that I can

withstand any physical pain. When I would work out and reach I point where I didn't think I could go on, I would reach back to my labor experiences and find the strength to do another ten minutes on the Stairmaster. If I ever do decide to go back to the gym, I'll have to keep that imagery in mind.

The point is, childbirth is not an experience I reveled in, but I got through it. I bought into the whole natural childbirth experience, huffing and puffing my way through contractions, suffering pain I thought should be totally unnecessary to bring new life into the world. When I finally succumbed to using a drug, it only took the edge off the pain but did nothing to remove the pain itself. What did help me was going into this experience with the expectation that this would be one bad day physically in my life to be rewarded by the most intense joy I've ever known. I was open to the experience, frightened but excited by the thought of having my babies.

Divorce with Dignity
Kathleen Berge Entenmann

During this time of intense external and internal
conflict, you too should open yourself to the experience.
If you develop a "batten down the hatches" or "hide in
the storm cellar" mind set, you may miss out on events
that will later serve you in other life struggles. This
doesn't mean that you become the village idiot, standing
in the middle of the town square with your arms raised
up to the sky as rain drenches you and lightning bolts
strike. You don't accept whatever abuse is dumped on
you without comment or possible retaliation. And you
don't hide in bed with the covers pulled up over your
nose, peeking warily at the world around you and
praying this is all a bad dream.

What you do is to find the courage within
yourself, or with the help of a competent professional, to
deal with the changes in your life and to *learn from the
experience.* Remember, if you decide to remarry, your
odds of that marriage failing go from 1:2 to 2:3. The
deck is stacked against you so you need to be armed with

as much caution and experience as possible to not repeat

the same mistakes. And if you find yourself repeating

the same mistakes, learn the how-to of correcting them

this time so that you will not end up where you are now.

This is tough stuff. It's extremely tough to look

upon this as somer learning experience when everything

in your world appears to be crumbling and you're

looking for something stable to hang onto to ride out the

storm. Be wiling to look beyond the old crutches to new

changes. Get off the bar stool and get on a treadmill.

Alcohol is the worst crutch because it muddles your

thinking and emotions and leaves you with empty

calories. Be open to new relationships, and I don't mean

romantic ones. Reacquaint yourself with neglected

friends and meet new ones (and not from the next bar

stool). Rediscover your religion and go back to church.

This is a great time to awaken your spiritual side in

looking for positive answers and direction. Just heed my

warning about the clergy as counselors: sometimes

they're not the people to lead you out of this particular crisis. But by all means seek comfort and solace in worship and prayer.

Another change you might want to consider at this time is a new career or change in career. Out of economic necessity you may find yourself back in the workplace, somewhere you didn't think you'd find yourself again. Given the current economic climate, a job search might be unrealistic so seek out the advice of a good career counselor, one who has their hand on the pulse of the job force. Beware of jumping at the first job that presents itself; that might not be the best alternative at this time. What you don't need is another failure to add to your list. You also don't need to add a narcissistic or demanding boss to the list of people you're dealing with in addition to your ex-spouse.

Just remember what I stated at the beginning of this step: where there is life there is hope. There is life after this divorce and how you live it will be your decision to make. Be prepared for the changes ahead: some terrifying, some painful, some comforting, some exciting. Be willing to move forward and act out of a sense of personal self worth that demonstrates what a true survivor you are and not a pathetic character deserving of pity or worse yet, contempt. Find the strength of character to change so that you thrive in your new afterlife following this divorce. Live as a person of dignity.

Tasks for Step Ten

1. Take time to assess yourself. Examine your strengths, weaknesses, needs and desires. Ask yourself if you're where you want to be. If the answer is no (and my guess is that the answer is no) then choreograph a plan of how to get where you want to be. Think seriously about money, relationships, character flaws, personal well-being. Start by changing the little things you can and then move onto the bigger ones. Congratulate yourself for each step forward you take, whether of not it works

out. Change isn't easy and the attempt is as important as

the result.

Chapter Thirteen

Samantha awoke in the bright light. It was Saturday and she had slept through the early morning hours. She jumped out of bed, refreshed and ready to start the weekend. Her plans included a trip to her new gym followed by lunch and shopping with friends.

The events of the past week were still swirling in her head. She and Ben were able to sit down and discuss all the issues they needed to resolve: house, assets, support, custody. She decided that the house should be sold and the proceeds divided when Edward graduated from high school. Until then Ben would continue paying the mortgage as well as college expenses for Cynthia. She would share in his 401k and they divided the stock portfolio. Her financial future was looking good, especially with Nick offering advice on investments and taxes.

She was already looking at the types of homes she hoped to own once the house she and Ben had built was sold. Her idea of a quaint Victorian in the middle of town was now unrealistic. She didn't want to spend the type of money she knew would be needed to maintain an older home. She was thinking about new construction by a reputable builder, preferably a townhouse.

Samantha also decided to begin learning French, a language she loved to hear. In the past she would occasionally throw out a few words or phrases, uttering a "mon dieu" instead of "Oh God." Somehow it didn't seem like blasphemy when spoken in another language. Learning a new language at her age was proving more challenging than she thought it would be, but practicing in a French restaurant was so delicious.

The kids were fine with the finality of the divorce, happy that both parents were still in their lives and would continue to be so well into the future. Samantha's family grudgingly accepted the news, but she wasn't looking for support from that corner of her life. She knew her sisters were happily discussing her "failure" with their mother, but so what? Long ago they had stopped being a factor in her life.

She and Jordan had a renaissance of their college friendship. Samantha was determined to keep this friendship alive and thriving. She repeatedly assured Jordan that her advice and support had been important to her during this time and she was resolved to be as helpful a friend to Jordan as Jordan had been to her. The exercise class was fun, especially with her best friend alongside her.

Samantha also decided to change churches. Reverend Dick seemed to direct his sermons at her in recent weeks when he spoke of the disturbing dissolution of the American family. Samantha knew the good reverend was not happy with her decision not to seek marriage counseling from him. The decision to change churches was also made easy when Edward and Cynthia wanted to start attending a youth group their friends belonged to at another Presbyterian church in town. They were already attending retreats and planning a mission trip to the southwest.

Next month Samantha would begin a new job teaching part time at a local trade school. One of Ben's friends taught criminal law there to future private police and mall guards. Her position was to teach business English. She was not impressed with the head of the school who was more concerned that she take attendance and adhere to the school rules on absences and tardiness than the substance of her teaching. In fact, she suspected that once she was in the classroom the school couldn't care less what she actually taught. Oh well, it was a job, something else to get her out of the house and into the mainstream of life. As soon as she began graduate school and started a teaching assistant position, she would be out of there.

After leaving off the kids at school that week, Samantha explored a small nearby town with quaint shops. In one craft gift shop she found the a beautifully framed quotation, perfect for the breakfast nook. As she sat at the small breakfast table, sipping coffee and contemplating her day ahead, she would read the Irish blessing:

May those who love us, love us.

And those who don't may God turn their hearts.

And if he can't turn their hearts may He turn their ankles so we'll know them by their limping.

She would now be on the lookout for the limping.

Divorce with Dignity
Kathleen Berge Entenmann

Divorce with Dignity
Kathleen Berge Entenmann

Divorce with Dignity
Kathleen Berge Entenmann

Divorce with Dignity
Kathleen Berge Entenmann

www.ingramcontent.com/pod-product-compliance
Lightning Source LLC
Chambersburg PA
CBHW072023190526
45166CB00015B/59